The Comm

Producer & International Distributor
eBookPro Publishing
www.ebook-pro.com

The Commandant's Dog
Shmuel David

Translation: Zoe Jordan

Contact: shmuelik7@gmail.com
ISBN 9798476214540

THE
COMMANDANT'S
DOG

SHMUEL DAVID

1

She lay on the ground and groaned in pain. Tom looked at her and froze where he stood. She could have been his grandmother. What was he supposed to do now, he asked himself. What had Dingo done? He had never acted out or gotten off his leash on previous walks around the neighborhood. Tom looked around for help. The woman went on moaning and gritting her teeth, trying to hold back her cries. Tom wanted to help her up, but she stopped him with her hand and warned him not to touch her. Aaron, the downstairs neighbor who always asked after Dingo, was alerted by the cries and emerged from his apartment. Within moments he was leaning over her and asking her where it hurt, but immediately realized that the situation was not improving and called 911 from his cellphone.

"We can't move her, Tom," Aaron explained. "We'll just stay here and keep an eye on her until the ambulance arrives."

The elderly woman was still writhing in pain. Tom, who was very confused and did not know what to do first — especially because he felt guilty — wanted to offer help to make up for Dingo's actions.

She pointed at her purse and said to Tom, "And you, young man, don't just stand there like a lump! Get my phone out of my bag and look for 'Amos.' Call him right now," she said, barely able to get the words out through waves of pain. Tom bent down to take the purse and look for the phone.

"Would you like me to bring you water? I'll run and get it now, okay?"

"No, no water," she whispered. "Just call Amos. Quick."

Tom found Amos in her contact list and called. There was no answer so he tried again and again.

"Where is that ambulance?" said Aaron impatiently.

"Maybe I should bring her water in the meantime anyway and take Dingo home?" Tom asked.

"Fine, but be quick," said Aaron. "You know who she is, right?"

"No, I don't know her," said Tom. "This is the first time we've met."

"This is Yula. She's a Holocaust survivor. A very special woman."

This information did not help Tom's mood or feeling of shame.

The ambulance sirens were approaching as Tom returned with a glass of water. Yula lay practically unconscious and was unable to drink from the glass. The ambulance stopped on the street right beside where she had fallen. The back doors opened at once and two paramedics took a stretcher out onto the sidewalk. Quickly and skillfully, they transferred Yula into the vehicle and asked Aaron what exactly had happened. Aaron pointed at Tom. "I didn't see what happened, ask him. He was here when she fell," he said.

Tom told them that Dingo had been running very fast and only barely touched her, hardly even made contact, and she fell. Tom was upset and said he was very sorry and that he could come with them to the hospital to help.

"No, no, there's no need," said the nurse as he took her pulse and blood pressure. We're off, but has anyone informed the family?" he asked before loading the stretcher into the vehicle. "We have to inform them now. Tell them to come to the emergency room at Tel Hashomer."

Tom remembered that he was holding Yula's cellphone, so before returning it to her purse, he copied Amos' phone number down and then set the purse with the phone down on the stretcher. The paramedics got up into the ambulance, one sitting beside Yula while the other closed the door. As quickly as they had arrived, they sped off, the ambulance racing, sirens howling, straight to Tel Hashomer Hospital.

***

When they first got to the apartment in Ramat Gan, to which his parents had moved them from their rural home in the Galilee, Tom was shocked. He couldn't imagine living here, in this grey, noisy place. No way, he thought to himself when he saw the little three-room apartment on the fourth floor. He was used to wide-open space, to the fields, yellow in summer, purple in spring, and green in winter. He wasn't the kind of kid you could confine to a little city apartment. He had grown up among the cows and turkeys that his father raised and was always surrounded by dogs, usually ones he had found in all sorts of places and adopted, to the dismay of his mother Eleanor, who was not inclined to country life. Eleanor was the one who had pressed for them to get out of the muck of the farm, which demanded all of their time and energy and scarcely gave them back anything in return. Tom thought his mother was only interested in comfort; she just wanted an easy life and lots of money. He felt that it was his father who would ultimately pay the price and have to sacrifice his values, just so his mother could say, "Great, I feel like we really improved our quality of life." She would say it with that funny 'r' of hers because Eleanor was originally from the United States and had moved here from Philadelphia or 'Philly,' as she called it.

Tom, on the other hand, did not feel that there had been any kind of improvement. On the contrary, he felt that he had been removed from everything fun in life. From the moment he got to the new apartment, he didn't like the place. He hated feeling shut inside a building with all those stories and was sure that this whole move from the country to the city was just to keep the peace between his parents. Maybe now they would stop fighting.

Tom's dad began working as an accountant at the Tel Hashomer hospital where he had to sit for eight hours a day, sometimes nine, in an office in one of those new buildings in the hospital complex. He didn't even complain that he spent most of his days in his little office in the new building, trapped under those neon lights and barely able to see the sun. Eleanor didn't complain either. She didn't mind being a medical secretary for some heart surgeon from America, making people's appointments and giving them their test results. The only thing that mattered to her was that now she could take the bus or her little Suzuki and go to a concert or show in the city if she wanted, and she was no longer mad at his dad for wasting all his time on agriculture. In the city, he could get a proper salary without worrying about poultry diseases or aphids on the grapefruits.

What infuriated Tom was that they didn't even consult with him about the move or consider him at all. He didn't even have any friends in the new place. He felt all alone in an unfamiliar world. Everything here required advanced planning. Instead of just wandering over to the basketball court and seeing friends, his mother had to sign him up for the basketball club, as if he were a little kid. Back home he was used to seeing the yard and all the fields spread out before him right outside the house. And if he wanted, he could always just grab his bike and ride over the train tracks to go visit his grandma, who was well-known and loved in the village, who lived in the little house shaded by the big eucalyptus trees.

But now? Grandma is in the ground, and Tom lives far away from the village and feels trapped in the little fourth-floor apartment. If he at least had a bicycle, like the other kids in his class, maybe he could meet friends and go places with them.

"There's no room in here for a bike," said his dad. "And if you lock it outside, someone will steal it."

So what do we have here? He asked himself. Apart from four walls and a view, as his mother was quick to mention.

"You've never been bored before," said his mother. "You always found something to do," she tried to encourage Tom.

"That's because there were always things to do," he replied. "Here there's nothing."

"So go find something. You could read books like you used to," said Mom. "You can write in a journal about our move to the city. You were always good at compositions."

But Tom wasn't in the mood for any of that. The best thing he had going for him was Dingo, his wild dog. At first, Eleanor had been firmly opposed to taking Dingo with them.

"Are you crazy, to make a dog, and a wild one like Dingo, live in an apartment? There aren't as many dogs as possible in the city, and city dogs are usually small and well-trained," she said, but she was wrong. There were plenty of dogs just on their street in Ramat Gan, even big ones, who lived with their owners in little apartments on upper floors. They were always taking them out for walks and to run around and burn off some energy. In the end, Eleanor was persuaded. Tom reminded her that Dingo had saved him once, that he wasn't just a loyal dog, but one who would do whatever it took to save his owner from trouble.

Tom would never forget that Dingo had saved him from a viper. Just as the viper was slithering towards Tom's bare foot, Dingo had noticed it. At once he sunk his teeth into its neck, near its head so it couldn't snap, killing the snake and saving Tom. Tom would never forget how his anxious mother stood there as he and Dingo returned home, with the dead snake dangling from the dog's strong jaws. Grateful and relieved, she had told Tom that he owed Dingo his life. Tom's father had gotten him Dingo for his Bar Mitzvah, and he may have been the happiest boy in the world that day. Dingo was a mutt: a Golden Retriever crossed with a Pointer. And between his spirit and his yellow-white color with grey spots, he reminded Tom of the wild Australian dingo. Because of his excess energy, Dingo needed to run around outside a *lot*. Now, in Ramat Gan, when Tom took him to the park or they ran some trail far from home, and he saw him happy and carefree, he too forgot for a moment that they lived in a little apartment on the fourth floor and was simply happy.

Tom would say that there are two kinds of people: those who love dogs and those who are indifferent to them. It goes the other way, too. There are dogs who would do anything for their owner, and those who like their owners just fine, but wouldn't follow them into the fire.

2

That night, after the incident with Yula and Dingo, Tom couldn't fall asleep. He thought about the conversation with Amos and worried he might think that Yula's fall was his fault. He was afraid that Amos would think he was to blame because he hadn't held onto the dog tightly enough.

"Dingo was so excited and he was pulling me," Tom had tried to explain, "I couldn't stop him," he tried to defend himself, but he realized that Amos wasn't interested in the details. He just asked where he should go, and when Tom told him to go to the emergency room at Tel Hashomer and offered to join him, Amos replied that there was no need; only close family members were permitted to visit.

During dinner, Tom was upset, and his mother couldn't help but notice.

"You look very depressed. Did something happen at school?" Eleanor asked.

Tom shook his head.

"You can tell us if something happened. Maybe I can help?"

"The upstairs neighbor fell," muttered Tom, barely moving his lips.

"And how does that concern you?" Asked Eleanor.

"Dingo knocked her over and I feel guilty, okay?" Tears slid down his cheeks.

"I'm sure it's not your fault. These things happen. She might not even be angry with you."

"But maybe she is, because Dingo is my dog and I didn't stop him."

"Why don't you calm down, Tom," she said, gently stroking his shoulder. "If you want, we can send her flowers when she gets home."

When Tom called Amos the next morning to ask about Yula, Amos sounded troubled. "She had an operation last night. She has a hip fracture," he said. "And she'll need to stay here in the orthopedic unit for a few more days, then ten more days of recovery," he added.

"How is she now?" Asked Tom.

"She's still under anesthesia, but when that wears off it will probably hurt again."

"I am so, so sorry about what happened. My dog was so excited he just bolted past her and wasn't paying attention. He barely touched her."

"I understand," said Amos, and Tom felt a little relief. "These things happen."

"When can I come visit?" Tom asked.

"Let's see how she feels tomorrow. She still can't have visitors today."

"Okay so maybe tomorrow. I'll call you to see if that'll work."

Tom was distressed throughout the school day. He felt that if he could only speak with her and explain what happened, and if she would only forgive him, he would feel better. His geography teacher commented that he looked lost in thought and not following what was happening in class.

"You're somewhere else today," he rebuked, but Tom's mind was wandering. He was thinking about what awaited him later that afternoon. It would be his first day going to the basketball club at the community center. He had been waiting for it for a few days already; his father felt he should have the chance to play a sport he loved and that it might take the edge off his loneliness here in the city.

That afternoon he called Amos again who said that Yula was on the mend. He could visit the following day on the condition that he bring an adult with him, since Amos wasn't sure that the hospital would let him into the ward alone. But Tom insisted that he wanted to come to see her as soon as possible and that since his father worked at the hospital, he could get him in.

The next day, Tom's father waited for him at the hospital entrance and then led him to the orthopedic unit. It was Tom's first time visiting the hospital itself, apart from his father's office, and he was surprised by how long the corridors were. *It's like walking through a maze,* he thought to himself when they finally reached the unit's double doors.

The doctor who admitted them told Tom, "You should be aware that this unit is less patients in pajamas lying in bed.

Lots of our patients in the unit are in casts up to their neck and you will probably also see limbs hung with weights from various contraptions." The young nurse who joined him and his father asked Tom if he was from Yula's family and immediately answered her own question, saying, "You must be the grandson, right? I can see the resemblance." Tom's father was quick to clarify that they weren't family but rather good neighbors.

When they peeked into the rooms as they passed through the corridor, they did see many legs hanging in the air and suddenly Tom was afraid that Yula would look like that too but when they reached room number 218, he was relieved to see her covered by a blanket with the hospital logo printed on it. Her left hand lay above the blanket with an IV drip connected to her spindly arm, a bandage holding the needle firmly to her skin. Her face looked good and she even smiled at Tom.

"Here is the young man. I knew you would turn up," she said in a soft voice. "You looked so miserable the other day. Even I felt sorry for you."

"Yes, I felt terrible when you fell. And all because of Dingo. He's a wild animal that one."

"Wild indeed," Yula laughed.

"I'm also very sorry for what happened," Tom's dad added. "I'm Reuben, Tom's father; we're your neighbors on the fourth floor." "Yes, I saw you when you moved in. You were so busy we didn't get the chance to meet properly."

"Tom is really a good kid, but he loves dogs so much. He treats them as if they were members of the family."

"I also love dogs," said Yula. "I have an interesting story about a dog that saved me, actually. He didn't knock me over," she smiled. "Amos already knows this one," she turned to her son. "It's the one with that dog, Ziggy, I called him, a Great Dane who belonged to the camp commandant. Well, anyway, it's a long story. Maybe someone will write it down someday."

"Tom here is great at writing stories. Actually, it's the one thing he really excels in at school, composition," said Reuben, who was standing impatiently. "Forgive me, but I work here in the hospital, in the treasury. I left my office in the middle of work and I have to get back," he added. "It was nice to meet you and see you looking well. I hope that we can get to know each other better, in nicer circumstances," he said and left.

"Before the story of the dog that saved me," Yula turned to Tom, "I really always loved dogs. Ever since I was little," she said. "So now I will tell you about my first dog or, more to the point, you can read about him because I've written about him in my notebook. It's of memories from my life in Warsaw. Here, read it, maybe you'll write about it sometime." She pulled an old brown notebook from her bag. The handwriting was cramped and slanted. She asked Tom to read aloud:

I was a child. Everyone called me Yula, except my mother and caregiver Irena, who called me Yulinka. We had a good life then, in those days before the war. Who was even thinking about war then? Since I was an only child, with my parents' and caregiver's full attention, I was pretty spoiled. The four of us lived in a big, beautiful apartment on Hipoteczna Street in Warsaw.

The summer when I was eight-and-a-half, the whole family took a vacation to the forest north of Warsaw, in the holiday village called Urle. We stayed in a guest house called "Higiena" that belonged to a woman named Helena who had a beautiful dog called Popsy that I bonded with at once. I would play with him and hike with him through the forest trails. Seeing how much I loved him, my father promised to get me a dog of my own.

When we got back to the city, I waited to see if Dad had kept his promise, every day when I got home from school; maybe the dog would be waiting for me. But day after day, there was no dog, and each day I felt disappointed.

I hate when promises aren't kept, but I trusted my father who, until then, had kept every promise he had ever made to me. Meanwhile, the summer ended and fall arrived and the yellow leaves fell from the trees and it grew cold outside, and still, I was waiting day after day for the dog.

At that time, I really believed in people and took them at their word. I also believed the old Gypsy palm reader that Irena, my caregiver, took me to. This happened during that same vacation in Urle, at the guest house. I still remember that visit. The old woman sat across from me with no teeth and the most wrinkled face I had ever seen. She took my hand to read my fortune and when she looked at my lifeline she froze, "You will have a long life, Yula." She even knew my name. She knew everything about me. "You will live until age ninety-three, and no matter what bad, hard things happen in your life, you will get through it and live until ninety-three."

Yula laughed and said, "But she wasn't entirely right. I'll be ninety-four soon and everyone is afraid I might not make it, but look, here I am, laughing with you. Up until now, every situation in which I seemed to be nearing my end — and I had many of those — I always remembered that promise and felt that someone up above was watching over me."

Tom went on reading from Yula's notebook:

...Much time has passed since that summer vacation. Autumn came and went and winter's snow arrived. Even Christmas passed. In our family, it was tradition to buy Christmas presents.

My father's family was totally secular, almost completely as-similated, and Dad would only go to synagogue once a year on Yom Kippur, and even then he only went because of my grandfather on my mother's side. He even had his own seat reserved in the Great Synagogue of Warsaw. I didn't go to synagogue either. I've gone maybe twice in my life for Simchat Torah, which was a happy occasion, when they danced with the Torah and threw candies.

Anyway, there was still no dog and I was afraid that maybe Dad had just said that, and maybe he was one of those people who made promises he never planned to keep. But then, one morning, I woke up in my cozy bedroom with all my dolls lining the window sill. Through the window I saw, with my eyes still half-closed, snow falling gently and piling on the tree branches outside. I had the feeling that someone was watching me, and when I opened my eyes wider and yawned a big yawn, I saw

Mom sitting on the edge of my bed and Dad standing beside her holding a little dog with white fur. He had a big brown spot on his head over one ear and another black spot on his back. I thought I was dreaming and yelped happily: "Dad! Mom! I don't believe it." And then, excitedly, "Give him to me, let me hold him, Dad, he's so sweet!"

Then I remembered that it was my birthday, and I was nine.

I was wearing my nightgown when I picked him up in both arms and held him tight to my chest. I felt his body heat and the sweet smell of his breath. I always loved dogs. I would see a stray dog on the street and bring it home but my mother always told me that now was not the right time. I so badly wanted a dog. Now for the first time I had one of my own who would live in my home and I would feed him and take care of him.

Dad told me that he was an English fox terrier and that his fur was coarse and curly, not smooth like the other kind of fox terrier. The breed received its name because the British used them for fox hunting. My dog was four months old, still a puppy, and Dad said that we had to look after him like a baby.

"I got him from a friend at work who is moving to America with his family," Dad said.

Mom added, "Everyone is going to America now. As if things here are so bad."

"There are people who see what's happening to the Jews in Germany now here too, and are starting to get scared," Dad replied. He then added, "We don't have anything to fear, for now. I have a good job and we don't want for anything."

I set my dog down carefully on the floor and saw how he

looked at me and turned his head from side to side as if listening for something with his big ears.

"What will you call him?" Dad asked me.

I thought for a moment, then said, "Iris. I will call him Iris." I remembered the book of Greek mythology which lay on my bedside table and the goddess of the rainbow I had read about the night before. It seemed like the perfect name for him.

Iris grew and was a handsome dog who loved people, children in particular, and he would run after me everywhere I went, apart from school or when I went with my best friend Barbara to a show or the circus. Later, when the Poles began to harass us, I felt safer walking with Iris than alone, even though he wasn't a particularly scary dog. In fact, he was even a bit of a coward, because when the terrible bombings by German planes over Warsaw began, he would always run and hide under my bed. Maybe he thought I could protect him.

I will never forget the day that the bombings began. The day before, Mom and I had gone to buy me school supplies for the fifth grade. We bought notebooks and pencils and a ruler: everything I needed. But the following day, instead of going to school, we hid under the beds and tables. Dad had already been recruited to the Polish army and Irena, my Polish caregiver, no longer worked for us. Iris' howls, along with my screams, drove Mom and Anya, her sister, out of their minds. Mom said it would be better for us to go live with Grandma and Grandpa on Pawia Street. There was more space there anyway.

Iris could hear the whistle of the bomb and would howl before it even fell. One day, when Mom went out to post a letter to Dad, in the army, there was a whistling sound and Iris howled and I screamed until Aunt Anya came out of the kitchen to quiet me. That turned out to be very lucky because moments later, the bomb fell and all the kitchens on that side of the building collapsed like dominoes.

Later, when we were living on Poznanska Street, at my other grandmother's house, I came home one day and saw that something was not right. Iris did not come to greet me as he always did, nor jump on me as I came in the door. I was afraid that something had happened to him. I saw Mom and Grandma looking grim, their eyes on the floor. They didn't want to look me in the eye when I screamed, "You killed Iris! Bring him back!"

Mom burst into tears. "We had no choice, Yulinka, I had to," she said. "He would have put us at risk."

"But how? Why?" I cried. "I loved him so much and he was having such a hard time with all of the explosions."

Mom said that it was precisely because he could not stand the explosions, and we couldn't explain it to him.

I ran out to the yard where I met Yanek, the son of the building's porter. He told me that he saw what happened, how Mom asked a Polish soldier, along with a group of other soldiers who were out in the yard, to shoot the dog. A few minutes later he had heard the shooting.

I asked Yanek to help me and together we dragged Iris to a spot where, until recently, there had been a tall building, on the corner of Jerozalemskie and Poznanska Streets, and now there was a large crater. Yanek helped me bury him there and put a big stone over the hole. With his little penknife, he helped me to *engrave the name "Iris" on a piece of wood, but we didn't know whether to put a cross or Star of David over the burial site. All I knew was that for the first time, I understood what people meant when they spoke of a place from which no one returns.*

3

Following his visit, Tom was relieved that nobody blamed him for Yula's fall and, apart from coming to see her twice a week, his life returned to normal. He made sure to visit when her family members weren't there. He came by bus, and the guard at the entrance, who already knew him as Reuben the accountant's son, let him in and directed him to the orthopedic recovery ward, to which Yula had been transferred. The atmosphere there was more open and welcoming. There were no longer cries of pain from injured patients or arms and legs suspended in the air. Here he saw patients with limbs in casts walking up and down the hallway or doing mat exercises in the training room. He found Yula doing well, engrossed in reading. Yula loved to read. Since childhood, she had spent lots of time alone with a book in her hands. She smiled at Tom as he entered.

"You're looking out for me, aren't you Tom?" She smiled. "You're my angel. I can't wait to get out of here and walk again," she said.

"How long have you been here?" Tom asked.

"Since yesterday morning," she said. "I've already had my physiotherapy for today and they said I can go out for some air in the wheelchair. I'll just ask a nurse to help me into a chair and then we can go. You'll push, right?" She asked. "Just go to the nurses' station and ask one of them to help."

A nurse seated her in a wheelchair and instructed Tom how to steer and brake. Then the two headed for the exit and out toward the garden. They stopped beside one of the benches along the path, and Tom sat down with Yula at his side in her wheelchair when a big German Shepherd ran past them, chasing after a smaller, yelping dog. The dogs rolled on the ground, biting and growling; it was hard to tell if it was playful or violent. Suddenly Yula let out the kind of lip-smacking 'tze-tze-tze' sound that calls dogs to attention. The two dogs stopped what they were doing and looked at her. She gestured with her hand to them to come and the big dog left the little one behind, head down, tail wagging and approached Yula. She stroked his soft brown fur and spoke to him. "Good dog, good boy." He sat beside her, letting her pet him.

"I see you really do love dogs," said Tom. "It's no small feat that a one who doesn't even know you, and a wild one like Dingo, would run over with his tail wagging, looking for affection. That says more about the person than the dog," he added, once again observing his theory of dogs and humans play out before his eyes.

"You're right," she said. "That's exactly what happened with me and the camp commandant's dog. Everyone was terrified of that dog, who was known for attacking prisoners, but I would just call his name and he would come cuddle with me. It's a special story and I hope you will write about it one day, my bond with that dog, and his owner too. He was a vicious man."

Yula recalled the first day she arrived at the camp and the commandant's introduction.

"His name was Rost, Dr. Rost. He ran the camp."

"What camp?" Tom asked, in suspense.

"It was called Skarzysko-Kamienna, one of the cruelest camps there was," she replied.

"We arrived one day in 1943 and there stood Dr. Rost with his enormous dog, a Great Dane who looked like a real predator. From my first glance at him I thought, this man with the lean, ugly face and thin, round glasses looks evil. But I comforted myself that he could not be so bad, since anyone with such a handsome, well-kept dog at his side could not be so cruel."

"But he really was, wasn't he?" Tom asked.

"After that terrible greeting, in the factory warehouse, where we were instructed to strip down completely and put everything we had onto a big blanket spread out in the middle, we still weren't sure. We felt uncomfortable undressing, even though most of us wore rags by then, not even real clothes. He went up to one of the girls, I think her name was Havaleh, I don't remember exactly, and screamed at her, 'Take everything off, all of it!' Then he took out his rifle. I couldn't believe what was happening before my eyes. He shot her once in the head and she fell to the ground as a trail of blood flowed from her forehead. Then he put the rifle back in its holster and said to the rest of us, 'Understand?'

"Let's go back now, I'm getting tired," she said to Tom. "Take me inside."

Tom was still stunned by what he had just heard. "Hang on, just let me catch my breath," he said. "What did you say the camp was called?"

"Yes, I know it's hard for Hebrew speakers to pronounce. Skarzysko-Kamienna," said Yula.

They went back into the hospital and a nurse helped her back into her bed. Yula said, "The physical therapist told me that tomorrow he will show me how to get in and out of the chair on my own, but in the meantime, I have to rely on others." Then she asked him, "Tell me, Tom, were you ever so scared that you wet yourself?"

Tom was surprised by her direct question. "Maybe when I was really little. Once we stole oranges from the mean neighbor's orchard. Everyone called him that because he had no problem giving kids a real slap. When he caught us red-handed, the others managed to get away but he caught me. I was so scared I peed a little in my pants. I knew what was coming."

"That's exactly the kind of fear I felt when I got to the hospital last week and they told me they would have to do an operation," said Yula. "And I was even more scared when, before the surgery, I had to sign a form and they explained that they would have to put me under. That scared me the most, it's a fear that's hard to explain. Even though all the doctors said it wasn't a risky operation, it reminded me of the day when I was paralyzed by fear, when I got caught out after curfew in Warsaw."

"I was your age at that time, fourteen, maybe even a little younger. I knew that it was forbidden to be out after curfew on Karmelicka Street, but it was an accident. I was returning home from selling Mom's clothes on the Polish side, outside the ghetto walls, and hadn't noticed that it was already eleven in the morning.

"Everyone knew that by eleven, trucks full of German soldiers would leave Pawia Street towards Karmelicka, which was usually bustling with Jews, in order to enforce the harsh curfew, and God help anyone who was caught. Just the thought of being lashed by their long whips was enough to send chills up my spine. The trucks would stop and the soldiers would get out, cracking their whips. They were maybe two meters long and let out a fearful snap when they hit the air or struck someone. They also had German Shepherds with them, meant to intimidate. I actually got along with the dogs, but the whips terrified me.

"When I heard the German soldiers shouting and the wails of people being whipped, I realized it was after curfew. I was scared out of my wits. I didn't know whether to run — they would most likely catch me and whip me mercilessly — or hide; there was a decent chance they wouldn't find me. But where? As the barking dogs and shouting soldiers grew nearer, I tried to think. I looked around and saw a pile of snow on the sidewalk that had been cleared off the street that morning.

With no time to think I leaped into it, as I was, scrambling with both hands to cover myself as much as possible with snow.

"I sat huddled inside the snow up to my neck, shaking with fear. What if they could see the pile moving? What if my head was peeking out and a soldier saw me? This was probably the end of me, here in this freezing pile of snow, and no one would know that I had disappeared. They wouldn't even remember that there had once been a girl who lived with her father and mother and Irena in Hipoteczna Street 3, who loved playing with her best friend Barbara. It occurred to me that I hadn't seen Barbara or Johan for a long time. In fact, since that day we had been told to pack whatever we could into a suitcase and leave our beloved home in ten minutes.

"We were in such a panic we didn't know what to take. They evacuated all of the apartments in the building, including Barbara's. This is what I was thinking about, there in the snow.

"The more time passed, the colder I became. I was sure that I would freeze to death. Or worse, they would find me and beat me to death, so my mother and Aunt Anya would never even recognize me. My father had been gone since the bombings over the city began, when he and Uncle Bruno, his brother, were drafted to the Polish army. But I thought of Mom, who complained that I made enough trouble for three children, saying it was lucky she had only brought one child into this cruel world. Before the war, she never said such things. Back then my mother was very well-mannered and always dressed in beautiful clothes from Gottesman's department store. Thinking of her from my freezing hiding place, I even forgave her for the time, back when we had a nice life, when people could go out and attend the theater, when she hadn't let me go to the Warsaw Circus with Barbara. I forgave her for everything. I recalled other visits to the circus, seeing the white giraffe and the tightrope walkers. I was so fascinated by them that I couldn't speak. My mind filled with thoughts until I forgot where I was, what time it was. But the time was after eleven in the morning and I was in Karmelicka Street in a pile of snow and at any moment, a chunk of it might fall away and expose me. I heard the whipping sounds and screams of the Jews that were caught and then suddenly, I heard nearby shouting in German: '*Komm her shmutziger Jude.*' [1]

"I thought he meant me and began to shake all over. Suddenly I felt something warm dripping down my inner thigh. I realized I had wet myself and began to shake even more, with shame and the fear that the urine might melt the snow or color it yellow and give me away.

"And then I remembered the old Gypsy woman's promise: 'You will live until age ninety-three,' she had said. I thought, why worry about a whipping? It might be terrible but it would pass. The important thing was that they not take my life, and since I already knew they wouldn't, I would be all right.

"Luckily for me, the sound of boots tramping on snow moved farther away, and then I heard the sound of a whip cutting through the air, immediately followed by the cry of

---

1   Come here, dirty Jew.

pain from a woman not far from me. I heard two more lashes and the cries turned into sobs which faded as the clicking of boots got farther away. At the same time, I heard the sound of the trucks approaching to collect the soldiers. Some thirty seconds later I heard the creak of the truck door as the soldiers climbed in, laughing and joking amongst themselves. With my German, I could understand exactly what kind of jokes they were telling.

"I waited a few minutes longer, huddled in my hiding place, until the last truck left and the street grew quiet again. I pushed the snow off quickly, enough to get out. There was a yellow stain at the bottom of the pile, evidence of the shameful state I had been in just minutes earlier.

"When they said they would anesthetize me before the operation, I felt paralyzed with fear. I felt like I did then, when I was terrified that the German soldiers would find me." Yula paused and asked Tom to bring her a glass of water. She took a sip from her glass, then looked at him and said, "It's late, Tom. Maybe it's time for you to go home?"

"You're right," he said. "I should go now before I miss the bus."

4

That evening when he got home, Tom was so agitated by the story of Yula's first dog that he ran straight to Dingo, petting him and promising that he would never let anyone hurt him. He heard a knock at the door. "Open up, please," he heard his mother. "Come to the table, it's dinner time."

Tom, who didn't usually tell his parents about his day, couldn't help himself sharing Yula's story of Iris.

"It's so terrible, her mom let them kill him," he said in distress. "I'll never let anyone take Dingo from me."

"That was wartime," said Tom's father. "Things were different. She could barely provide for herself and her daughter, let alone a dog. She was being responsible," he said, taking another piece of pickled herring from the jar and putting it on his plate.

"Dad, remember Mickey, the mule I used to ride?" asked Tom.

"How could I forget our crazy mule! Have you forgotten how he once knocked you over when he jumped the creek?" His father asked in response.

"I remember," said Tom. "I also remember when our neighbor Avigdor put a bullet in his head when Mickey got hit by that truck."

"Yes, but you're forgetting how much he suffered after the accident. It was heartbreaking to see him like that," said Reuben. "You brought him food and water, but in the end, he wouldn't even eat."

"I was so mad at you when they took his body. You didn't get it. But I stood out behind the shed and watched it happen. I saw Avigdor raise his gun and aim it. Then I closed my eyes and heard the shot."

"I remember that you took it really hard," said Eleanor. "And that whole incident was hard for me too. But we're here now." As if wanting to change the subject, she asked, "Say, Tom, do you really want to write down Yula's memories? Dad said it seems like there's a really interesting story there. Is that so?"

"I think so," said Reuben. "You could record her with your phone. There must be a good application you can get for recording. You probably know how to find one better than me; maybe next time she tells you stories you can record her."

"Excellent idea," said Eleanor. "But you have to ask her permission, you know. It's not just good manners, you need her consent. She might not want to be recorded." When he got to the orthopedic recovery ward at Tel Hashomer the next day, Yula was already sitting in her wheelchair. She no longer needed help getting from the bed into the chair and back. Now she was doing short trips down the hall with her walker, but in order to go for a walk outside, she needed a companion. Tom had his phone ready in recording mode.

"It's good that you came," Yula said, pleased. "I was just waiting for someone to accompany me outside with my walker."

"But inside you can walk on your own?" Tom asked. "What's the difference?"

"Outside there's less supervision and the sidewalk is uneven. So it's harder to push the walker but I have to keep practicing," she said. "They're teaching me lots of exercises. It's interesting comparing the treatment here to the injury I had in Majdanek. Did I tell you about that?"

"No, you didn't. But before you tell me I have to ask you if you would agree to something…" He wasn't sure the right way to ask and he was anxious about her response.

"What is it?" Asked Yula. "What are you being so mysterious about today?"

"Nothing mysterious, just something I thought could be helpful if I really do wind up writing your story."

"Well, what is it? You're keeping me in suspense," Yula said impatiently.

"I just wanted to ask if it's okay if I record you while you're talking, so that I can listen to it again later."

"What, didn't I give testimony at Yad Vashem?" She said in surprise. "They recorded me too, but it was more of a question-answer format, like a TV quiz," she said. "When I talk to you I feel more free to just tell my whole story. Anyway, I don't mind if you record me or take notes, whatever you want."

"Thanks, Yula. Where were we?" Tom asked before immediately answering himself, "You were starting to tell me about the injury you had in Majdanek… which was what?"

"That was before I got to that hellish camp, Skarzysko-Ka-mienna. By the time I got there, I already had the wound in my thigh. We were still at Majdanek, it was morning and I desperately needed to use the latrines, which were right behind our barracks, a row of holes in the ground with low walls around them, made of blocks, not even high enough to hide or maintain a little modesty. They watched us even there, in the latrines and the line for the latrines. There was a watchtower every fifty meters staffed by German soldiers. That morning there was a long line and as I was waiting, I suddenly felt a searing pain. I was stunned. At first, I didn't realize that it was a bullet, and it was only when I touched it with my hand that I understood that my leg was bleeding like crazy. I fainted. They took me to the hospital at once, which was managed by Polish doctors — they might have been polit-ical prisoners — who took very good care of me. The wound was in my thigh and reached all the way to the colon. You can still see the hole in my thigh," said Yula, pointing at the leg which had been injured in the most recent incident. Tom felt another wave of guilt.

"The wound was big, nearly a quarter of my thigh was missing. It took a long time for it to heal. That's that story and now the same poor leg has taken another hit. It's my bad luck, it's really not your fault. It could have been a car accident, or falling down the stairs; it just happens that it was your dog that caused it. But I'm glad you are here with me, I really don't want you to feel guilty."

Yula and Tom walked another fifty meters or so, taking slow, measured steps until they stopped beside a bench in the shade beside the walkway.

"Oy! You have no idea how tiring this is for me. You are young and healthy and everything works. Your generation is so lucky you will never know what we went through in Europe," she said when they sat down. "Ah, I promised I would tell you how I survived Skarzysko-Kamienna, but first let me tell you about the introduction when we arrived."

Tom pressed the record icon on his cellphone.

"It was summer, the beginning of August. The sky was cloudy as if it might rain at any moment. I was seventeen by then, in the midst of my lost youth, and I wept over my bitter fate. I found myself standing in that lineup, undressing, with other women and girls like me. A moment earlier, the commander had shot one of the girls, just like that, just to frighten us, and indeed, I shook with fear. My mother was standing beside me and I saw that she was shaking too. Only five hours earlier we had been in the yard at Majdanek, sure that it was the worst possible place, and yet here we were in an even worse place, and we still didn't know what awaited us.

"At Majdanek, before boarding the crowded train car, we were transferred from one field to another where there were men too. Among them, we saw Bronek, Dad's brother. When he asked Mom if she had seen his wife or their young son, Mom couldn't stop herself from bursting into tears and the two of them broke down and wept on each other's shoulders. I cried too. I remembered how at Majdanek, on the way to work, I saw mothers locked in pens with their little children. My aunt, Bronek's wife, was among them with their little son Djishu. They sat crammed together, awaiting their sentence. They were there for a few days and then disappeared. The camp's veterans, those who had been there for some time, whispered the terrible word: crematorium. We parted ways from Bronek and the Polish officers hurried us into the densely packed train.

"Anyway, when I was lying in the Polish hospital with my gunshot wound, a senior doctor came over to me one morning and told me that Majdanek's hangman wanted to speak to me. This time I thought my end had come. How much longer could I hang onto the Gypsy woman's promise that I would live until age ninety-three? I had been spared a few times already, surely this time I wouldn't. The hangman probably wanted to tell me that I was no longer useful and there was no choice, patients must be disposed of.

"But when I went to see him, I was met with a surprise.

"'I hear you through the wall of my office all day. You have such a fine and pretty voice and your German is very good. Are you sure you weren't born in Germany? Dr. Michaela said that you're Jewish, is that so?' He asked.

"'Yes, that's right, I'm from Warsaw,' I told him, embarrassed. 'But I learned German at school when I was little. Polish school.' Then he said something surprising: 'it doesn't matter that you're Jewish, I spoke with Dr. Michaela and asked that they take good care of you, but I want you to stay in that room close to me so that I can hear your voice.' I was pleased.

In the evening, when my mother came to the window to visit me, because visitors were not allowed inside the rooms, I told her in a whisper of this encounter and added that he had promised to help me when I was better and left the hospital. Mom was so happy. But he didn't say how awful the place he would send us on to would be. At least we weren't going to the crematorium. I didn't know what was better. He was the hangman that everyone feared, and a doctor, apparently. He was responsible for the selections — deciding who would live or die — as well as the hangings for anyone who tried to escape. I stood there swollen with hunger. I weighed about thirty kilograms at that time and had the gunshot wound to the thigh that had not yet healed. I saw him send people in better shape than myself to the incinerator and I was sure that I had no chance in this selection but he remembered me and kept his word.

"Back at the new camp, we were exhausted, standing in that humiliating introductory ritual for a long time and when it was over, the guards surrounded us from all sides and hurried us along, shouting, "Move it, let's go to the bunks.' We walked for kilometers, our legs and souls depleted, as the officers prodded us, 'don't stand there, keep walking.'

"When we reached the barracks, a large sign at the entrance indicated 'Barrack C' which we later learned was the worst of all the labor divisions. And if we thought our initiation a few hours ago had been demeaning, we were in for a surprise. Now the real show began. As we stood there, an overseer emerged from the division office followed by a majestic young woman wearing riding boots to above the knee and a white raincoat. In her hand, shaking with impatience, she held a leather whip. All of the officers stood up straighter as she passed, awaiting her orders. She turned to us and said, 'I am your new commandant in the hardest division of the camp: C Division.' She addressed the men in a slightly sanctimonious tone. 'It all depends on you, men. If you work hard we will see to your needs.' Then she turned to the women, most of them young and pretty, and said in a degrading tone: 'And you, whores, where did you come from?' Of course, she didn't wait for a response. Later, we learned her name, Mrs. Markovicova, the terror of the whole division.

"Then the officers began to force us into the barracks, pushing and prodding us with their batons. That was when we first saw what awaited most of us in a few weeks' time. That's how we will look too, I thought to myself with growing horror. The people inside looked like shells of human beings, like figures wrapped in paper, the skin of their faces red or yellow, though it was not yet clear why, and the hair on their heads thin to nonexistent. They sat or lay on their filthy bunks with no mattresses or blankets. At Majdanek, there had at least been blankets, which we also used to keep warm at night, to pad the hard wood that pressed against the flesh until it hurt. Here the bunks were bare, the upper bunks had no ladders to climb onto them, and the barracks were as crowded as a chicken coup. At least they separated men and women, I thought to myself.

"Everything was done quickly, out of fear of the guards. The fat, crude guard that took us to our barracks was actually nice and didn't threaten us. He understood that Mom could not climb up to the upper bunk without a ladder so he ordered her onto a lower bunk and me to the one right above her.

"I tried to find a position that wouldn't hurt, so I could fall asleep — who knew what the next day would bring — but I couldn't. I felt sorry for my mother, who I heard breathing heavily below me. My mother, the delicate, pretty woman who so loved to dress well and wear red lipstick, now had to lie on a hard, filthy bunk with no blanket. She, who caught everyone's attention when she walked by, dressed in her beautiful clothes and her silver fox fur thrown over her shoulders as she returned from the kitchen to the card table on Sunday evenings, now had to huddle in the cramped bunk with dozens of other women, dressed in smelly rags.

"I thought wistfully of Majdanek, where we hauled rocks all day from one place to another but at least at night we were able to sleep. I tried to turn over and change position but because it was so cramped, pressed up against the next girl, my turning over forced all of my neighbors to turn with me.

"I couldn't stop recalling the horrific sight of Hanaleh, that young woman the guards had forced to undress to ensure that she wasn't hiding anything in her clothes, and that bastard Rost who shot her because she refused to comply. I must have said something out loud because I heard Mom sighing beneath me. 'That's what awaits us, daughter. We would have been better off staying in Majdanek. Some favor he did us, that hangman of yours...' said Mom in a broken voice, 'Not that it's your fault. Who could have known? You wanted us to stay together, but we never imagined this could be such a terrible place.'

"I hoped that my mother really didn't blame me. Eventual-ly, I must have slept soundly because suddenly I saw the white giraffe just beside me in the Warsaw circus tent. I was stroking her long legs and looking up to the top of the tent, where her little head looked as though it were sailing through the sky.

"Back then Barbara and I went to the circus together on Saturdays. The two of us sat in the back seat of her father's car, while her parents sat up front. Barbara's mother was tall and elegant in a boater hat over her styled hair, her fox fur over her shoulders, and Barbara's father had broad shoulders and his summer hat on.

"When I woke up, my back hurt from sleeping on the hard surface and I remembered the dream. I hadn't seen Barbara for a long time, since we were forced out of our apartment on Hipoteczna 3. Neighbors said that they had tried to escape. Later I saw her for a moment during a cruel selection in Um-schlagplatz. I was so tense from the cries of the mothers whose babies had been taken and my grandmother who suddenly fled that I barely spoke to Barbara. I just told her that I was looking for my grandmother and little Felusha, my cousin.

"I was sure that Barbara's family would not be taken to the square. I knew her from the Polish school where she stayed on after I had transferred to the Jewish school. Hers was a very wealthy, well-connected family, with expensive furniture and sculptures in their living room. I would go to their house often to play with Barbara, and she once told me that they had an estate north of Warsaw but her father had sold it because he wanted to live like everyone else in the big city.

"It was still dark outside when the guards began shouting their wakeup call, '*Apell*, into formation!' The shouting was accompanied by the thumping of their batons on the bunks; I was very far indeed from those childhood experiences. It seemed I would never see a white giraffe again. "Come, Tom, it's gotten chilly. We should get back to the unit," Yula suddenly snapped out of her reverie and gave Tom a melancholy smile.

5

Yula got home a week ago. Tom had been busy with basketball, but even busier with schoolwork. He had to improve his grades in math, his worst subject. After the last parent-teacher meeting, he promised his father that he would try harder and if he still didn't do well, he would take the private lessons that Reuben suggested. He saw his father struggling under the burden of making a living, working long hours and sometimes staying at the office late into the evening. His parents didn't even go out together much or allow themselves luxuries.

"Getting coffee with a friend is not considered a luxury," Eleanor would say when Reuben complained about it. He couldn't complain too much because she contributed her part by working at the cardiologist's clinic in the afternoons. Given their financial situation, Tom didn't feel comfortable burdening them with the further expense of a private tutor. The day Yula returned home, Tom went out with Dingo for an after-school walk and saw an ambulance parked beside the building. Two paramedics carefully transferred Yula in her wheelchair from the back of the vehicle onto the sidewalk. Tom hurried to greet her. Amos and one of his children were there too and helped her to the elevator. After welcoming her home, Tom promised to visit the following afternoon.

The next day, Tom and Eleanor showed up with a cake and a bouquet of flowers. Eleanor introduced herself and apologized for the incident and Yula assured her that everything was back to normal and there was nothing to worry about. On the contrary, she felt blessed to meet this sweet, principled young man who had enlisted to help her and keep her company.

"Well here is another sweet thing," said Eleanor and placed the cake on the kitchen table.

They spoke a little longer before Eleanor apologized, saying that she had to go. Yula turned to Tom and asked, "You'll stay, right? I have more to tell you. This time I will carry on without the notebook. It helps remind me of events and I'll keep it here next to us, maybe I'll reference it. But I enjoy talking to you more than reading from an old diary like some Holocaust remembrance day ceremony…" Yula laughed to herself. Tom smiled and said he would be happy to and gently asked again if it would be okay for him to record their conversation. Yula said it was fine and instructed Tom where the fridge was, saying he could take some apple juice or water for himself to drink. He began recording and she resumed her story. "Early in the morning there was shouting: 'Everybody out! *Appell! Appell!*' At that point, I did not yet know that '*Appell*' meant they were counting everybody. They were always counting. 'Why do they care so much how many of us there are?' I asked

Mom. 'After all, we're like flies here. They put us to work, put us to death, as they please.' I still didn't understand that the most important thing was work. Each person was just a tool for them and if they were short on manpower, the machines wouldn't have people to operate them.

"During each '*Appell*' there was a selection: left to the firing squad and right to go on living for now, but working to the limit of human capacity. At the first *Appell*, they divided us into work units. Schmidts, a young, handsome man, walked among us. He assessed each of us with his sharp blue eyes, and if a woman appealed to him, he gestured that she come over to him. Schmidts' unit was known as the 'privileged group' and he always chose the youngest, prettiest women for his unit. Work in his unit was easier than that in the rest of the C camp, which was considered the worst of all the factory camps. The work involved filling caps for 20-millimeter anti-aircraft shells. Mom, who was still pretty, and I were chosen for his unit as soon as we arrived. The rest were sent to the picric acid unit. At that point, we did not yet know why there was no need for a crematorium here. They didn't even really need the firing squad, a camp veteran told Mom. People died working, as they breathed in the toxic fumes of the picric acid.

Mom didn't want me to hear that. She herself wanted to plug her ears when she heard how toxic the picric acid and trotyl were. 'The picric acid workers have three months at the most,' she whispered to Mom.

"Right after the headcount, we began to march in dense rows with the guards moving us along, pushing and jabbing with their batons. It was a long way, nearly an hour's walk. Luckily it was August and the weather wasn't bad. The roads were not yet covered with snow. When we reached the factory, we saw all the others, including the picric team, the *pikriners* they were called. We were scared, afraid to look at the human skeletons with their yellow, peeling skin. Those who inhaled the poisonous fumes had sparse hair on their heads, which took on a reddish color. Those who worked with the trotyl, which was no less dangerous, also had yellow, peeling skin.

"'You are here to work. Sharata, the overseer will come momentarily and give you precise instructions,' Schmidts explained. Unlike Rost, who would yell instead of speaking, Schmidts explained quietly. 'Whoever works well, will live,' he said and added a warning, 'but anyone who does sloppy work, or does not meet the quota that we set, or produces too much *'schmaltz'* — defective product — will die.'

"I was terrified that I would not meet the quota, that they would find *schmaltz* among my work. That was how they forced us to work hard. Death hovered over us at every moment. But what happens when you stop fearing death? That's what happened with little Rivka, who had come to the camp in our transport but was not chosen to work among the privileged. On the day that Rivka found out what had happened to her parents who had been cruelly ripped away from her in her town of Poniatowa, she burst out screaming and ran straight toward the fence. It was an electric fence that would electrocute a person to death if they so much as touched it. Other girls held her tight so she couldn't run but she kept screaming that she wanted to die.

"Sharata, the work manager, gave us instructions on the right way to fill the preprepared caps with the explosive material and explained what was considered *schmaltz*. For instance, if we put too little explosive material in the cap, then the shell would not explode properly and if we put too much, it could cause accidents. We began to work. We were a group of around twenty women who had been chosen by Schmidts, and by contrast to those who produced the explosive material and worked with the picric acid, our work was clean. We packed the completed shells into designated boxes, with each shell in its own socket in the crate. We didn't notice time passing until we felt evening come on, but nobody thought to bring us food. We went on working, without any breaks, and only very late did a German-speaking supervisor show up with two loaves of bread, which looked more like two clumps of mud and were as black as coal. 'A loaf for every ten of you,' she said. 'Divide it amongst yourselves.' We had to measure how much each woman received and began to argue about who got more. I swallowed my bread without so much as chewing. Mom tried to tell me to save a little for later because who knows what would come and when they would next feed us.

"In the evening, we returned the same way we had come. This time from the factory to our sleeping quarters. We passed through the gate, beside which was a well-maintained barracks, unlike the rest of the camp. 'This is the white house,' the veteran woman told Mom. 'That's where Mrs. Markovicova lives. She brought her whole family here,' said the woman, who looked like a ghost. The sparse hair on her head was reddish and her nails were mangled. 'The barracks just to the left of it is her brother-in-law's, that bully Eisenberg, the one she appointed as chief of the guards. He's a man of the underworld, husband of her poor sister. He cheats on her with all of the young Polish girls at the camp. Only rarely, like at the reception of a new transport of prisoners, does Queen Markovicova come down to us, the hungry, exhausted prisoners. What you saw when you arrived was that once-monthly appearance,' she said with contempt. 'Sometimes she comes down to the people just to see their admiration for her in their hungry eyes, and she might throw some bread or a bit of chicken wing.'

"When we got back, hurting and exhausted to our barracks, we were met with the strong smell of disinfectant and urine. The 'latrine' was right behind our barracks, open to all and without any doors for privacy. The hard, dirty bunks awaited us, without so much as a mattress or blanket, on which we had to sleep after a full day of work, ten or more hours with no rest.

"But of all of the hardships, the hardest was the hunger, eating hardly a slice of bread for the entire workday. Back at the barracks in the evening, before even sitting down for a short rest, the guards once again began to hurry us with shouting and batons, this time for the distribution of soup. How disappointed we were when, once again, we had to eat like dogs, licking food from the bowl. My dog, Iris, at least had a bowl and he only needed his tongue to eat. Not only did we not have a bowl or cup, we didn't even have a spoon to bring the thin liquid to our lips. People passed around dirty old tins and we sipped directly from them.

"Suddenly, we heard the galloping of a horse from the direction of the gate and within a minute, the creaking of hooves was beside us with a cloud of dust over our lukewarm soup. The horse stopped and we saw its rider, the chief of the guards, Eisenberg, in all his glory. He tightened the reigns, one hand holding a big baton while the other rearranged the hat on his head. He had fake insignia pinned to his shoulders and he bellowed: 'we have discovered sabotage in the grenades department!' His voice echoed to the heavens. 'We know there are three people involved. We know who did this and they will be sent to the firing squad tomorrow morning,' he announced, then gave a command: '*Appell* in ten minutes in the usual place!' Everyone was frightened and scattered to their respective corners, each fearing for his life. Those who did it would not likely admit to it and others, who were innocent, would be put to death the next day.

"It was an especially tense and nerve-wracking count. In addition to Eisenberg who sat, as was his custom, on the horse, Mrs. Markovicova was also there in her high boots and whip, and of course Rost and his enormous dog. The charge was smuggling functioning grenades into crates designated for schmaltz and hiding them in the forest to be given to the partisans.

"I shook with fear and could feel my mother trembling beside me. At least it hadn't happened in our division.

"Rost passed between all of the members of the grenade division, and when nobody came forward, he pointed at three individuals, then gave his dog a command: 'Mensch – get that dog!' He pointed at a tall man wearing glasses, who shrieked hysterically as the dog began to drag him from the row. In that moment, Mrs. Markovicova intervened, shouting, 'stop, he's not one of them!' Everyone was surprised and Rost resumed scanning the crowd, only to choose someone else."

Yula cleared her throat and indicated that she needed a moment.

"Could you get me a glass of water?" She asked, stopping her story. "There, my water filter is on the counter. There are glasses there, take one for yourself, too." Tom stopped the recording. He filled one glass of water and brought it to Yula. "Why didn't you take one for yourself, too?" she asked.

"I'm not thirsty yet," said Tom.

"Ah, so good," said Yula after the first sip. "Just water — you don't need anything more than that." She took a deep breath. "Where were we?" She asked and Tom pressed the recording icon on his phone once more.

"I struggled to fall asleep all night and I thought of the tall guy with glasses who by some miracle had been saved from the firing squad that was meant to take place the following morning. But what about the other three?

"In such a situation, it's good to have someone to share your fears with and it bothered me that I was alone there; I had no one I could talk to. I thought I might befriend the other girls in my group, but they made me feel unwanted. From the very first day they had talked amongst themselves about me, maybe because I came with my mother, or because I didn't speak Yiddish? They ignored me and called me a snob. A Jew who doesn't speak Yiddish is hardly considered a Jew. I felt that all of the girls were excluding me and suspected that they switched from Polish to Yiddish when I approached or tried to talk to them.

"Mom felt lonely, too, but it didn't bother her as much. She was more troubled by hunger. She knew a little Yiddish from her parents, who had been more traditional. My grandfather even observed the Sabbath, and her parents spoke Yiddish together. My mother would translate for me. Before we went to sleep, she told me what they were saying about the tall man who had been saved today. His name was Handel, he was a very talented medical student and the son of the famous Professor Handel of Lviv University. She also told me that Markovicova was actually a Jew from the city of Skarzysko's well-known Gutman family. The father of the family had died some time ago, leaving the mother and three daughters. One was Markovicova, who had always been the black sheep of the family. They married her to some student whose life she had made miserable. She hit and abused him until they separated and then she married another man, Markovic, whose name she took, who had been a member of the Judenrat and was killed by the Gestapo. She got to the camp on account of her negotiation skills, which she learned when she was trying to save her husband from the Gestapo. She could sweet talk German officers of every rank and had thus infiltrated the camp. Only later did she bring her entire family, including her young niece Relia, who she was trying to set up with one of the Jews at the camp.

"As I was listening to Mom, there was a sudden noise and a commotion broke out. The Polish guards shouted, 'catch him, he's getting away!' It was Meir Goza, from the picric division, who was supposed to be taken out and shot the next morning. With nothing to lose, he had broken out through a window of the *pikriners'* barracks beside ours. The guards' frightened shouts and the barking of Rost's dog, also recruited for the hunt, could be heard from all directions.

"I couldn't sleep for a long time. I thought of my father and the cruel abuse he had endured before his death. Mom lay on the bunk below and asked me why I wasn't sleeping and I told her that I missed Dad. She sighed deeply and said that she missed him too. I thought that it was good that he couldn't see the suffering we had been through at Majdanek. Maybe he was even lucky that he had avoided this hell.

"I thought of the good times before the war. Even though he worked long hours in the power plant where he had an important role, he always took good care of Mom and me. He would buy Mom beautiful jewelry and fox fur, and he had brought me Iris, who was with me up until the war when he ultimately went mad from the bombings. Dad would take my hand in his and we would walk around the pretty park beside Poznanska Street, and he took Barbara and I to the zoo. We loved walking around on Saturdays and seeing the monkeys and the sleeping lions. Mom didn't like coming with us to the zoo but she went to concerts with Dad a lot. He had the patience to sit and help me with my math homework when I had difficulty and he encouraged me to read. He would always bring me adventure stories for children and by fourth grade he bought me a book of Greek mythology. In the camp, I sometimes imagined that I heard his voice beside me, particularly during headcount when I heard anger in his voice, 'Leave the girl alone, what do you want from her?'

"I thought of that terrible morning of April 1942. Dad had been missing for a few days, when suddenly a Gestapo car stopped beside the house, according to Sonia, the neighbor who was outside just then. They threw a man, who was covered in blood and barely recognizable, out of the car. Hearing Sonia's cries, people gathered. Mom and I also hurried downstairs, and only after the man turned onto his back so that his face was visible did Mom and I see the worst thing imaginable: Dad's contorted, bloodstained face. All of his front teeth were missing, which distorted his face and made it hard to recognize him. I screamed first. It was hard for me to keep the horror inside even though Grandma always tried to teach me that I would do well never to get hysterical. But how could I hold back when my father was nearly dead before my eyes? And not two days passed before he died at home of his injuries. We couldn't help him. Not even the kind doctor that Bronek, who worked for the police at the time, brought from the Chista Hospital could help. He told us that Dad had a day, maybe two to live. He was hemorrhaging in his lungs and his stomach so bad that even surgery would no longer help.

"We buried him in the Jewish cemetery in Okopowa, and after that I wanted people to leave me alone. I found a quiet place in the cemetery, close to Dad's grave. There I would sometimes sit for entire days, and think about everything: what had happened to our family and what else might happen, though even in my darkest nightmares I could never have imagined Majdanek much less Skarzysko-Kamienna. I thought about Dad, who had gone to the place from which no one returns, and I thought about this cruel world and the unnecessary war that made good people like him suffer so much.

"I think that in the end, I fell asleep and couldn't remember if I had dreamed about Dad or thought of him before falling asleep."Morning came and again it brought the beating of batons against the bunks and shouts from the guards to hurry, 'Everyone out! *Appell! Appell!*'"

6

On the day that Tom returned home from basketball bruised all over, he couldn't hide that something had happened. The cut above his lip was still bleeding and the blue mark under his eye was fresh and swollen. Although Tom did not like telling his parents what was going on in school or with friends, his face was evidence that there had been trouble.

It all started when he and Mikel, his Filipino friend from the basketball team, began spending time together. There were others who saw their friendship and didn't like it. The two grew closer until one day, Tom invited Mikel over to his house. Mikel appreciated the gesture but for some reason was afraid to say yes or no. In any case, the two went to Tom's house the next day. Tom had talked a lot about Dingo and Mikel was excited to meet him and take the dog for a run at the park.

Mikel went to a different school, in South Tel Aviv, the rougher part of town, but he joined Tom's team because he showed real promise and his trainer recommended that he join a team with a professional coach. Adrian, Tom's basketball coach, played for the national team and was a certified youth coach. Mikel and his mother were at risk of deportation from Israel. Even though she had worked in the country for a few years already, she was considered illegal, he told Tom, since her work permit was no longer valid.

Mikel was a smiling, friendly youth. He wasn't tall but made up for it with speed and agility and could sink a basket from almost anywhere. The other boys on the team nicknamed him "the Filipino hotshot."

On the day that Mikel's mother received notice that she would have to leave the country within two weeks, Mikel didn't show up for practice. Tom, who already knew about the constant threat of the immigration inspectors, began to worry, and during the break, he called the emergency number that Mikel had given him, a number that he should only call under special circumstances. He reached Susan, Mikel's mom, who said that Mikel was afraid to go out because of their immigration status.

"Can I speak with him?" Tom asked.

"What's your name?" Susan asked.

"Tell him it's Tom from basketball."

A few seconds passed and Tom heard Mikel's dejected voice.

"You don't get it, Tom. They'll catch me and put me on a plane."

Tom couldn't believe it. Could it be that in our country they would deport a boy who had grown up here and spoke Hebrew like an Israeli, since birth, and was just like him, because of his background and the fact that his mother's work permit had expired?

"But they know your address, don't they? They could come any time," Tom tried to understand.

"No. We aren't at our apartment anymore," Mikel said. "Mom has a friend who took us somewhere else."

"So why don't you come here? You can live with me in the meantime. You can stay in my room with me," Tom said, and added, "Everyone here on the team, including Coach Adrian, we all care about you, Mikel, you can't just disappear on us."

When Tom told his parents his suggestion that Mikel come and stay with them, they grew anxious. "Tom, you're putting us in an awkward position," said Reuben, who was a child of Holocaust survivors himself, and no stranger to persecution. "You think I take it lightly? What you're telling me, about Mikel and his mother is terrible. Especially in a country that was established by people who suffered so much from being different in countries that didn't want them." Tom had heard this many times before. "But you have to understand," he said, unconvincingly, "it's a legal matter. We can't break the law, right?"

Eleanor was also unwilling to host Mikel. "Not because he's different, on the contrary," she said. "I don't mind if you're friends and hang out together. But living with us? Sleeping here? That would make us collaborators. With all due respect to your friend," she said, "I wouldn't want the immigration police banging on our door in the middle of the night and find Mikel here. How would that look?"

Tom heard them but refused to believe that his parents weren't willing to help. They just said how terrible it was but wouldn't do anything about it themselves.

"Fine, I'll manage," he said. "I will invite Mikel over for the afternoon and in the evening he will go back to his hiding place."

Reuben and Eleanor agreed to that. "An afternoon visit won't be considered hiding an illegal immigrant," they said. Tom put on Dingo's leash to take him out for a walk to the park. He knew that his parents would always rather play it safe and be law-abiding citizens rather than help someone in distress, so he found a partial solution.

From the park, Tom phoned Mikel's emergency number again. "Prepare your school bag with notebooks and basketball clothes for practice and come play basketball tomorrow as usual. Afterward, we'll go to my place. You can hang out there, we'll play with Dingo at the park, and you can do homework in peace and eat dinner, okay?" Tom told him. "Afterward, I will walk you to your bus."

Tom waited for Mikel's response, and when he heard the hesitant "yes" he was pleased. The next morning, Mikel showed up in his athletic wear and school bag just as they had agreed. It was a particularly good practice and Mikel did well. He actually smiled a little. Even Adrian noticed the difference and praised Mikel's playing. After the game, as the two boys headed to catch the bus to Tom's house, some older guys intercepted them, swearing at Mikel and shouting that he go back to his country. "What do you want here in Israel?" they said. "This country is for Jews only." Tom tried to protect his friend, shouting back at them, but one of the guys tore Mikel's backpack off his shoulders. Mikel tried to fight back but it was no use. The attacker dumped the contents of the school bag on the ground. When Tom saw this, he went into a fury, punching him with all his might, but the other two bullies caught Tom by the arms while the third hit him in the face. Then they moved on to Mikel, pushing him down hard. He fell and hit the sidewalk and the three ran away and disappeared. There was no one there to witness or stop them, but Tom recognized the youngest of the three bullies. Tom and Mikel sat, stunned and beaten, at the bus station. "I recognized Kobi's face. All three were wearing hoods, but I recognized his face," said Tom with difficulty. It hurt to speak. "He's in the grade above me at school." Luckily a woman came along and when she saw them she gave Tom a pack of tissues to stop the bleeding.

"Here, put this on your lip and put pressure on it," she told him and placed the tissue over the cut. She also suggested that they go straight to the first aid station but Tom thanked her and said that they would go home first.

When they got home, Eleanor noticed Tom's bleeding lip and was very frightened. "What happened? Where were you? Come, we're going to the hospital! Now!" She shouted hysterically. "And who is this friend of yours? Is this Mikel that you told us about?"

"Yes," said Tom. "Mom, this is Mikel," he said and in the same breath tried to calm her and said that there was no need to go to the emergency room. But it was no use; Eleanor would not calm down.

"The two of you into my car, now!" She ordered. Tom ultimately agreed but Mikel begged to stay home. "I'm barely hurt," he said and showed her that he just had a few scratches on his arms where the attacker had pulled his backpack.

"Mikel will stay in my room until we get back," Tom suggested. "We don't want them to identify him there."

When Tom got back with one stitch and a bandage over his upper lip, he found Mikel sitting in his room, focused on a math problem. Tom suggested he come along to take Dingo for a walk and Mikel was very happy to get some air. When they got home, they met Yula in the stairway. Tom said hi and Dingo ran straight to her to get some affection. Tom introduced her to Mikel, his friend from basketball, and told Mikel about Yula, "This is Yula. She's a Holocaust survivor who has been through *a lot.*"

Yula noticed the bandage on Tom's face and asked what happened with concern. Tom told her about the three bullies and the violent assault.

"That's awful," said Yula. "It's so sad that in our country, people who suffered so much persecution, just for being Jewish, are now persecuting others. And it doesn't matter if it's about religion or anything else, that's no way for people who suffered so much and who declare themselves an enlightened, liberal people to behave. It's just shameful."

Tom saw that Mikel was eager to get going and he still had to walk him to the bus stop.

"So why don't you host him to stay at your place? At least for a few days."

"I can't. It's a long story," said Tom. "Not everyone wants to take the risk."

"Oy. Stay another minute. I have an interesting story that I remember well and it relates to what you just told me." Tom decided that they could stay long enough to hear the story and managed to get out his cellphone to record her.

"Following the Great Aktion, in July 1942, they got rid of the ghettos, both big and small. They grouped us in apartments in the famous Mila Street, though it wasn't Mila 18, of which Leon Yuris wrote in his famous book, but rather in number 7 or 9, I don't remember which, along with my aunt's caregiver. After some time, my aunt and cousin decided to move to the Aryan side of the city where it was safer, if you had a place to hide. The Poles didn't really like hiding Jews. They didn't even like it if another family in the building hid Jews. If caught, it was punishable by death, to the whole family and sometimes even everyone in the building. I decided that I wanted to go over to the Aryan side too. I had an address for my aunt Anya and she arranged for me to live with a friend of hers at Plac Unii Lubelskiej. I looked Aryan enough that I didn't have any problem walking around Warsaw with the Kennkarte papers that had been arranged for me. When I saw that it was reasonably safe on the Aryan side, I invited my mother to join me but after three days, informants caught and threatened her. The informants were Poles who gave up Jews to the Gestapo. At first, they just threatened to do so, and later they really did inform the Gestapo so that the presence of Jews would not endanger the building's residents.

"After her encounter with the informants, Mom was scared. She didn't want to take any chances so she returned to the ghetto. I remained alone in the apartment at Plac Unii Lubelskiej until one evening, returning from walking in the street and about to go up to the apartment, the doorman told me, 'I suggest that you not go up, the Gestapo are looking for you.' I turned and fled to my aunt who was living not far away, but in the meantime, there had been informants at her place too who had taken lots of money and valuables. I decided that I would also go back to the ghetto.

"We stayed there, Mom and I, until the next Aktion, in January 1943, which was much smaller than the first. There were no longer many Jews in the ghetto.

"But what am I doing, I promised I would tell you about that terrible camp, Skarzysko-Kamienna. You asked me last time and we didn't get to it, but I'll tell you some other time; it's late already," she said, petting Dingo. "And I'm glad to have met your friend Mikel. I really hope, Mikel," Yula turned to him, "that the immigration officers will realize that they are wrong, that it's a terrible injustice, and that you will be able to stay here in Israel."

"Thank you, Yula," said Mikel. "Up until now I had only heard about the Holocaust at school, and I couldn't really imagine it. This is the first time I've heard about it from someone who was actually there." Tom accompanied Mikel to his bus stop, which would take him to South Tel Aviv. On their way, they passed a corner store, just as an older man with a well-groomed little poodle passed by and began to bark at Dingo. Tom realized at once that he should get Dingo away from him before the two started to fight. He tightened the leash as much as he could, but it wasn't enough. When the yapping dog got near him, Dingo couldn't help himself and attacked him. Tom pulled with all his might, but when the dog's owner bent down to pick up the poodle to save him, Dingo bit him on the leg.

Not even a bite, Tom reported afterward at home. You could barely even see any marks on his skin. Tom grabbed Dingo by the collar at once and dragged him away, forcefully, but it was too late. The man began to scream that he was irresponsible and one shouldn't let a dog like that into the street without a muzzle. He asked Tom for his parents' names and address and threatened to sue them.

When Tom got home, Reuben looked at his face and said, "I heard from Mom what happened and now I see… It doesn't look good."

Tom's face was black and blue. The bandage covered his upper lip and the bruising under his eye had spread.

"Really, Dad, it's nothing," said Tom and immediately told them about the man that Dingo bit and his overreaction.

"It's not the bite I'm worried about," said Reuben, trying to comfort Tom. "Don't worry, I'm sure nothing will come of it. He patted his son on the shoulder and added, "What worries me more is that fight you and Mikel had with those guys, maybe they're criminals," said Reuben.

"Yes, Tom," said Mom. "Dad's right. I think you need to be more careful."

"What do you mean by that?" Said Tom. "To not hang out with Mikel anymore?" He asked angrily.

"We love you very much, Tom," said Eleanor. "And maybe I got a little hysterical when I saw my son bleeding from the mouth. I am, after all, your mother, and it hurts me to think of you getting beaten up."

"And you're hiding things from us again," said Reuben. "Like when we were living in the countryside and you were always doing pranks. But these aren't childish antics anymore, this could be dangerous."

"You're always blaming me!" Tom fumed. "As if I'm guilty for everything that happens. Then you're surprised that I don't tell you anything."

"We're not blaming you, sweetheart," said Eleanor, stroking his head as she tried to reason with him. "We worry about you. There's a difference."

"But believe me, Mom, it really wasn't my fault," said Tom, "They started it. They didn't like me going around with Mikel."

"Just promise us that from now on you will share with us more," said Reuben and pushed his plate away, indicating that he was done eating. "Promise?"

"Promise," said Tom and gave him the thumbs up. "But you don't have to worry so much about me," he said and pushed his chair back to get up from the table.

"Especially you, Mom," he said, as he brought his plate to the sink. "I'm not a little kid anymore."

7

Three days later, Reuben received a call from the Ministry of Health. They informed him that the following Monday, Dingo would be taken to the nearest pound to be quarantined for ten days to be sure that he didn't have rabies.

When Tom heard this, he ran and hugged Dingo as if to protect him. "My poor boy, poor Dingo," he whispered. "You are going to jail. But I will make sure to visit you," he said and put on Dingo's leash before taking him out for their evening walk. On their way, they ran into Yula, sitting on a bench. She was happy to see them.

"Great, I see that you no longer need the bandage and the cut will probably heal soon," she said. She was with her caregiver, Zoya, who came every day for a few hours to help her at home and for a bit of a walk outside. The memory of being attacked with Mikel was still fresh in Tom's mind. In particular, he thought of Kobi from the grade above his who had joined the bullies and he promised himself that he would teach him a lesson.

"And how is Mikel, does he still have to hide?" asked Yula.

"Yes, a few more days until the date they said that his mom must fly back to the Philippines. But there's a big anti-deportation demonstration this Thursday, at Habima Square. Mikel and his mom will be there too. And some important people will come to show their support and I organized friends from my class to come too," said Tom. "This is the first time I'll be at a demonstration."

"Great," said Yula. "I see that you are a good boy and want to help your friend in trouble. I recognized that in you back when you came to visit me at the hospital."

"Did you want to keep telling me about that camp where you were? Skarzysko something… I can't seem to remember the name," Tom asked with a smile. "It will also distract me from other things that are upsetting me lately," he added.

"Sure," Yula was pleased. "If it interests you, of course I will. The camp was called Skarzysko-Kamienna."

As usual, Tom took his cellphone from his pocket and turned on the recording function.

"You must think that we produced shells and mines for the Germans that would help them in the war without any resistance, but you should know that there was also great opposition. In autumn of 1943, there were rumors that they might transfer all of us to another camp and close this one. Most mornings, after *appell*, was the terrible walk to the factory where the kapo kept an eye on us the whole time, making sure that we walked in orderly rows. We were hundreds of prisoners walking, some struggling to stay on our feet, some skeletal, with hair falling out and yellow or reddish skin. We knew what awaited us at the factory: standing another ten hours on our feet and making sure that the exact right amount of explosive material went into each shell's cap. I was so scared to make any trouble – you know, any kind of sabotage – to hide defective shells, the kind they called '*schmaltz,*' inside the crates of the good ones, that kind of thing. But my friend Zhota, who I was very close with by then, told me that she did.

Zhota didn't care that the other girls were excluding me because I didn't speak Yiddish. She was a bit older than me and had fought in the Warsaw ghetto uprising with Mordechai Anielewicz's men, she said. She was brave at the camp too and would take good shells and put them into the crates of schmaltz – as instructed by Capo Lolek who was involved in the smuggling – to be taken to the forest and from there to the partisans. This was very dangerous, and in the end, of course, someone reported it. It was terrible. One Pole, who I think was called Kovalik, initiated the smuggling. He was caught and held along with Lolek. Rost immediately investigated the sabotage and two more collaborators were caught and put to death.

"Any kind of sabotage required great courage, as Sabina also told me. I knew Sabina from the second day of our time at the camp, but she was in Camp A, with the picric acid, and her older sister, Shoshana, looked out for her as if she were her daughter. 'Look after Sabina,' the girls' mother had instructed Shoshana before she was torn from her daughters. Those three words were etched in Shoshana's mind like a divine decree.

She would protect her sister at any cost.

"Sabina admired the courage of Shoshana, who would mix the defective shells in the same crate as the good ones. That was one of their secrets. She lived in perpetual fear that if the work manager ever discovered that she produced too much *schmaltz*, he would punish her. But she so wanted to do something, even something small, to feel that she was doing her part to disrupt the German military supply and even the little that she did eased her conscience. 'It's for my mother and father,' she whispered to me."

Yula took a short break and asked Tom to accompany her with her walker to the nearest street corner and back to the bench. She had promised the physiotherapist from the rehabilitation unit that she would continue her exercises at home and asked Zoya to wait for her on the bench until the two returned. Tom walked with her, taking small steps as she walked, and was pleased to see that she had made a lot of progress since they had last walked together.

"I see that telling me your story is particularly hard for you today," said Tom when they got back to the bench and sat down. "Shall we take a break?"

"It's fine, Tom," said Yula. "Come, let's look at my notebook again. Remember it? The one where I write the most important things that I want to be remembered, like for example about Rost's dog." She took the brown notebook from her bag and leafed through the densely written pages until she got to the right one and asked Tom to read:

Dr. Rost, the camp commander, would come to supervise at almost every selection. He came with his enormous dog, a dog nearly the size of a pony, with its huge, scary face but kind eyes; I was not afraid of him. We would stand in Appell *and this dog with its black spots – back then I didn't know that kind of great Dane was called a Harlequin – would come and sniff around the prisoners. I would call him to come, clicking my tongue and signaling with my finger. Everyone would look at me when the huge dog wagged his tail and stood beside me, rubbing his big head against me and licking me with his long wet tongue. I was so thin then, I weighed thirty-two kilograms, and he could easily have knocked me over just by turning his head. Even Rost was surprised that there was someone who wasn't afraid of his dog, who was meant to frighten and threaten the camp's prisoners. For some reason, I called the dog Ziggy, even though his name was Mensch – meaning 'man' in German slang. In fact, whenever Dr. Rost wanted the huge dog to bring him a Jewish prisoner to abuse, he would shout, "Mensch, get that dog!" When he said 'mensch' he meant the dog and when he said 'dog' he meant a Jew standing in* Appell. *He didn't know my name, but for some reason, he called me Lily. Maybe I reminded him of someone else.*

That was how it went every time we stood in Appell. *Everyone stood in line, shaking with fear that Dr. Rost would sic the dog on them, and Ziggy, when he wasn't obeying Dr. Rost's orders, would come to me for some affection. It bothered Rost, who probably wanted Ziggy to strike fear into the hearts of those standing there, while I petted his big head and back and called him pet names that I invented for him. I liked calling him Ziggel, or Ziggelman. And so a great friendship began between me and that huge dog. At the end of most workdays, when we returned to the camp, Ziggy would be standing by the barracks, waiting for me. In our third week at the camp, we saw Dr. Rost's dog in action for the first time. We stood in* Appell *as usual when Rost suddenly screamed, "Mensch, get that dog!" Dr. Rost was constantly calculating the number of workers against the number of shells, mines, or grenades that needed to be produced. He had a little notebook in which he must have calculated how many Jews he needed to kill today, or the opposite. If he was short on workers, he needed to know how many to add. Maybe he needed a new transport? Maybe they should freshen up the ranks of the exhausted workers and replace them with stronger, healthier ones.*

The moment Dr. Rost shouted, there was a frightening silence. Everyone was afraid that the dog would come to him and everyone but me shook with fear. I just hoped that he would come over so I could pat his big head again. But Ziggy would do as his master ordered rather than come to me for attention. Just like that, he transformed into a monster and pounced on the victim that Dr. Rost pointed to. The unfortunate man's cry pierced the silence. This time it was little Shime'le from the picric acid division who, it was rumored, had helped Meir Guza, the one who had escaped through the window that night. Shime'le helped him hide afterward and even distracted the guards during the escape. Dr. Rost had decided to take him out to be shot so that everyone would see, to make an example of him. Shime'le was almost lifeless when the dog ran up to him, sank his teeth into his flesh, and dragged him, bleeding, the length of the path. The dog did not release him until he was at his master's feet, and Dr. Rost called to the guards. "Take this away," he shouted, pointing at the bleeding Shime'le.

Having completed his task, Dr. Rost turned to the huge dog and stroked his head lovingly, showering him with praise and affection, "Good dog, what a good dog." Then he gave him a slice of sausage from the bag he carried with him.

The spectacle ended with the guards dragging Shime'le to the truck from which we heard the cries of other victims. They knew where they were headed: to the place from which no one returns. When Shime'le had been put onto the truck, Dr. Rost raised his voice. "Understand, Jews? Now, to work." We began our walk, terrified, toward the Hasag factories.

On the way to the factory, others talked about how the next transport was meant to come in October. Whoever was still alive then might be transferred to another camp. The veteran who walked with Mom told her that that's how they always did it. One transport comes, another goes, and every time there are rumors of the liquidation of the camp or renovations of its buildings.

When we got to the factory after our walk of more than an hour, we were greeted by Arno Weisselder, the work manager for Mr. Schmidts, who handed over most of the work to the acting inspector, the Polish Sharata, who was relatively decent and didn't abuse or beat the prisoners. He also made sure that we received our meal on time, and thanks to him they also added an additional bit of soup to the meal. In other departments, like the picric acid unit, they only got the bread that reminded me of mud.

During an outbreak of lice at the camp, we had to go through the disinfectant showers where I ran into Sabina again. We were excited to meet again even though it was hardly a happy occasion. The showers, at least, were not gas chambers, of which we had already heard rumors, but the humiliation was indescribable. I stood beside Sabina as they instructed us to undress. There was almost nothing to remove since our clothes were barely even clothes, sometimes just paper bags with a hole at the top to put your head through. At that point, I wore no underwear and just a rag that there was no point in disinfecting. Sabina had some scrap of fabric for a dress. They ordered us to put our clothes to one side and after they were disinfected we would collect them from the other end of the showers. I remember the feeling of shame and humiliation to this day. Mom was also forced to undress beside me, bearing only the faintest resemblance to the beautiful body she had possessed, which dwindled and withered with the hard work, food shortage, and poor hygiene at the camp.

I pitied her more than myself, and it hurt me to see her humiliated like that.

In the showers, we felt worthless, trying to maintain our last shreds of humanity. The girls tried to hide their most private parts with their hands and hurried inside, just to get through the nightmare as fast as possible.

When we got out and put our disinfected rags back on, Sabina said, "you're so lucky that your mother is here with you. Mine was killed before we got here." Then she told me about the abuse her sister had experienced a few days earlier when she tried to find a little peace and quiet in the bathrooms of the factory which were cleaner than the camp facilities. It wasn't just her, there were a few other girls also hiding in the bathroom for a few minutes to have a drink of water.

"Suddenly a guard, known to be a cruel sadist, came in. He shouted at all of them to get out. "Escaping your shift? Get out at once!" They scrambled to get out of there as fast as they could because then he locked the door and began to beat whoever remained. Shoshana was hiding at the back of one of the stalls which he opened angrily and started hitting her in the face with a pipe. Shoshana nearly fainted but he kept hitting her. Her mouth filled with blood and then she felt something hard in her mouth: teeth that had fallen out. She shouted, "My teeth! Leave me alone!" It was only when he saw the blood spurting from her mouth that he stopped.

Somehow she made it back to her work station, to her shift that she was forbidden to leave for even a moment. She returned to her machine but could hardly stand on her feet. Without teeth in her mouth, she looked like someone else. From then on, Shoshana's good heart remained, but her face was completely distorted.

"She's not here today," Sabina went on. "They took her to the hospital, maybe to save what they still can. I was so afraid at first when they told her that she wasn't going to work this morning. You know, because the ones who don't go to work in the morning, they're usually no longer with us by evening."

Yula closed the notebook and sighed. "I miss Sabina so much," she said.

8

That night, Tom had a hard time falling asleep. In his mind, he saw the skeletal prisoners with yellow, peeling skin and red, thinning hair. They worked with picric acid and trotyl and would not live more than three months under these conditions. How could they live at all? Tom thought. The idea of knowing that one's end was near but that one had to keep on working made him shiver, and if for any reason you did not go to work one morning, you would be replaced and by the next *Appell* and Rost's dog would come for you.

Tom remembered that Yula had told him how, because of the great risk of working with picric acid, there used to be strict rules forbidding shifts of more than eight hours, and there had been orders that the *pikriners* get special, additional food. But that had been at the beginning when Poles still worked at the factory. As soon as the Jewish prisoners came, and the agreement was signed with the Hasag arms company managers, the protocol changed and the *pikriners* worked twelve-hour shifts and received the same amount of food as everyone else.

In the morning, Tom got out of bed, still thinking about the camp. He went into the kitchen and saw his father in his chair, reading the morning newspaper as he drank coffee before work.

"Dad, what's picric acid?" Tom asked, expecting a response or some expression of recognition, but Reuben looked up from the newspaper at his son.

"You look tired, Tom, I see bags under your eyes," he said in a worried voice. "Have you not been sleeping well?"

Tom stretched his arms out to his sides and yawned, "Yeah, Dad," he said. "Why do you think I asked you about picric acid? I can't stop thinking about Yula's stories. At night I see the *pikriners* that she told me about, the ones who were exposed to all the toxic fumes. And I want to understand it better. I tried looking in my chemistry textbook but there wasn't anything in there and Google had lots of information but not much about how it affects people."

"Wait a second, where's Mom?" Tom asked, suddenly noticing that Eleanor was not at the table. "She didn't come say 'good morning' to me like she usually does."

"Mom went to a pilates class at the community center," said Reuben, "Which makes me the only one in this family who hasn't signed up for any kind of athletic activity yet," he added as if angry with himself.

"As for picric acid, sorry Tom, but I don't know, this is the first I've heard of it. It rings a bell, like maybe some kind of ingredient used for making explosives," said Reuben.

"And people really die from it?" asked Tom.

"Only if it explodes," said Reuben. "If it explodes you could definitely get injured or killed."

"No, no," said Tom, "I mean, if you breathe it in."

"Why don't you ask one of your teachers? I'm sorry, but I don't know any more than what I just told you," said Reuben. He then added in a concerned voice, "Apart from that, it worries me a little, this storytelling with Yula, maybe you are getting too involved… And it's interfering with your sleep."

"It was your idea, Dad," said Tom. "Remember when she was in the hospital and you suggested that I write her story sometime? Now I'm hooked, I can't just stop. I'm especially interested in the stories about the commandant's terrifying dog."

"Fine. Meanwhile, you look after your Dingo," Reuben smiled. "He's a little terrifying himself!"

Tom put Dingo's leash on him, showering him with affection and calling him pet names, as if Dingo knew that today was the day he would go into quarantine. Tom thought he should give him an extra special morning and took him for a long walk to the dog park where he let him run around with the other dogs, off-leash. When they got home, Tom gave him a bigger helping of kibble than usual and told him that it would just be a short time apart and that he, Tom, would be waiting and thinking of him for the whole ten days. When it came time to go to school, Tom insisted that he accompany Dingo to quarantine, even if he missed his first class. He had to come and see what kind of conditions they would keep Dingo in. His parents tried to talk him out of it, but it was no use. Reuben had to go to work and Mom, who was back from pilates by then, agreed to take him along to say goodbye to Dingo. "It's just ten days," said Reuben on his way out the door. "Nobody will kill him, Tom, relax."

Tom resumed his research on the chemicals Yula had mentioned. While Google didn't offer much useful information, he found out that trotyl was related to the famous explosive 'TNT' or, its proper name, 'trinitrotoluene.' Because it was not highly reactive, it could be placed inside a metal shell without exploding during its preparation, but when activated it was very powerful and stable enough to reach its target. Trotyl's uses were discovered in 1891 by the German chemist Karl Hauserman. It was known for its characteristic yellow color, which dyes anything it comes into contact with. Tom found nothing regarding its health implications.

Tom thought about who he could ask at school but his classes that day were geography, linguistics, history, and English, and he figured that a physics or chemistry teacher would be a better choice. Then he remembered that he had robotics club in the afternoon. He would try to ask Gilad, the robotics teacher, who might know a thing or two. Gilad was reliable concerning matters beyond robotics. He was probably older than Reuben and had kind eyes that were always smiling. Tom had heard from others at school that Gilad was an electrical engineer who did security-related work. He taught at the school for ideological reasons, to contribute his knowledge and experience in electronics and programming to curious youths. The school robotics program was part of an initiative by an American organization, 'First,' which also held competitions between schools for the fastest, most efficient robot. The finals were held every year in the United States, in Hartford, Connecticut.

Tom was excited about the subject right away; he loved the idea of building a robot. Gilad suggested that their group build a Roboner, a robot that can navigate a maze and uses sensors to avoid the maze walls. The Roboner's task was to find the room with a lit candle, extinguish it, and make its way back to where its journey started.

It was Tom's math teacher who recommended that he join the club. It would give him a fun, social introduction to the basics of programming. At first, Tom had to familiarize himself with new concepts like sensors, algorithms, the programming language 'C' and 'bugs,' those glitches that sometimes kept the group at the lab until late into the evening. But Gilad took it upon himself to bring Tom up to speed, staying with him after the rest of the students left to do additional programming exercises. Not everyone in the group was at the same level anyway. Eviatar, who was an expert programmer, was ahead of everyone else and led the sensor programming. He was a computer and mathematics genius and had helped Tom with math problems on more than one occasion.

That day, while Eviatar's team was busy dealing with a problem in one of the Roboner's sensors, Gilad sat with them, offering assistance. Tom took advantage of the opportunity and asked him, "Gilad, do you know what picric acid is?" Gilad was very surprised by the question. He appeared thoughtful, as if he had just been reminded of some terrible thing that had once happened to him.

"Where is this coming from all of a sudden?" He asked anxiously.

"I am helping my neighbor, a Holocaust survivor, write up her memories. She keeps mentioning picric acid and nobody can tell me what it is. Even Google," Tom said simply.

"Don't tell me she was in Skarzysko-Kamienna," said Gilad.

"Yes, yes, exactly, there, Skar... Skaz..." said Tom excitedly. "So you know about it?"

"Of course," said Gilad. "Do you think your neighbor would meet with me? What did you say her name was?"

"I didn't say, but her name is Yula and she has horrifying stories from there."

"I would really like to meet her. I also have an interesting story from there."

"But you're too young," Tom was taken aback. "You couldn't have been there."

"No, no, I wasn't there as a prisoner. Not at all. Talk to her, if you can, I'm sure she would be interested to hear a story of someone who was there under completely different circumstances."

"But what about the picric acid?" Tom didn't let go. "Is that really the stuff they put in the shells?"

"More or less," Gilad replied. "It's actually Trinitrophenol, a very strong acid, and prolonged exposure to it can cause severe damage to the mucus membranes, the respiratory system, the skin, and the kidneys. The skin dries out and turns yellow or red. Anyone working with it shouldn't be exposed for more than three or four hours a day and needs special respiratory protection and special food to reduce the likelihood of physical harm."

"Finally an explanation. Up until now, nobody I asked knew anything."

"And another thing. The acid was mostly used during the second world war. It is no longer in use, among other things because of the terrible damage it causes to anyone who comes in contact with it."

"I knew I asked the right person," said Tom. "How do you know all this?"

"Some general knowledge, but I also read a book called "The Yellow Death," which describes exactly what happened there."

"So I see I'm not the only one interested in this. I thought of writing a story about it. But I don't know if anyone would want to read it," said Tom.

"Come on, everybody," Gilad addressed the students that were trying to solve the problem. "Did anyone find the cause of the problem?"

"I think I know what happened," said Eviatar, pointing at his computer screen which displayed the program. "Here, see this 'if statement'? I think this condition cannot exist," said Eviatar. "I fixed the program but we haven't checked it yet, we have to go back to the start."

"Good job, Eviatar," said Gilad. "So what are you waiting for?"

"You," everyone answered in chorus and Gilad looked embarrassed.

When he returned home from school that evening, Tom found Yula on the bench beside the building. She was surprised to see him without Dingo. He told her that he had taken Dingo to quarantine that morning, and how miserable the dogs there looked. "The saddest part of the whole story is that Dingo looked so forlorn. He doesn't understand why he's stuck in a cage, and I don't know how he will manage with the conditions in there."

"It's unpleasant, but at least it's just ten days. Not the end of the world. For me the end of the world was at Skarzysko-Kamienna," she said. "You remember the notebook that I showed you? I'm trying to write my memories from that time but it's hard for me." She showed him the brown notebook and asked, "Could you just record me and afterward write it down like you did back in the rehabilitation unit?"

"Sure," said Tom. "Today we'll make it a bit short, I just have to go home, get my backpack and say hi to Mom and I'll be right back."

When he came back down a few minutes later, Yula was still sitting there waiting. "So back to the camp?" She asked, as if preparing herself. "I can't believe how clear my memories from there are. As if it hasn't been seventy years," she said. "Today I will tell you about the explosion in our department." Tom pulled out his phone and pressed record.

"It was winter, and our day began with the long morning walk over snow-covered roads to the factory. When you work day after day, hour after hour filling shells, the work becomes practically automatic, and you stop paying close attention to what you're doing. You just make sure to keep meeting the quota, and not produce too much *schmaltz*.

"When I told Sabina about my fear of the quota, she told me she also had nightmares about it. Like me, she worked automatically, nothing existed for her while she worked except opening the device and pouring in the substance, always pouring. In the beginning, the overseer would yell at her constantly: 'Pour faster, pass it, open it, device, pour, close it, pass it on, faster, faster, faster!' The devices would pass by her eyes at lightning speed and the press that produced the explosive picric acid cubes rumbled and screeched. 'Fast,' the overseer would shout at the workers, 'others have already filled four crates and we barely have two, come on.'

'I had this nightmare,' said Sabina, 'of three pairs of eyes staring at me, as if it was all my fault that we weren't making the quota. I was afraid to look at them, shaking all over. The quota, the quota. Eleven crates, each with one hundred and fifty cubes, and all of it to be done in one night. I felt that my strength had run out, I couldn't find the opening of the device, I forgot to clean the lid, they yelled at me, 'Why didn't you clean the lid? It could explode!' I woke up drenched in a cold sweat. The supervisor's words were still echoing in my mind and I thought that if there was an explosion I would be blamed and then I envisioned Rost's terrible dog running right at me to take me away. I leaped from my bunk shaking, in time to start a new day of work.'

"One day there was a disaster. It was at the work station of one of the girls not far from me. Probably the shell was already full when it fell to the ground. Suddenly there was a booming, deafening sound. The girl who had dropped the shell fell too, with blood covering her face. Two other girls nearby – luckily for me it didn't reach me – were badly hurt. The three injured girls were taken away on stretchers to a first aid station with a German doctor. The girl who dropped the shell was pronounced dead and the other two were badly injured. One of them, Esther, was a pretty girl who had come on the same transport as me and Mom. I even spoke with her a few times. She was in the same barracks and her bunk was three over to the right from mine. They said she was in bad shape but still alive. The doctor shouted at everyone to get back to work, and I stood shaking beside my machine barely able to set down the shell that I had just filled. I was in a panic that it would blow up in my face.

"Not far from us stood the cart of corpses, harnessed to the horses. There were three such carts, one for each camp. When they filled up, the horses would take them to the forest nearby to be burned.

"Out of the corner of my eye, I kept checking what was happening at the first aid station, which was not far from me. Eventually, I saw two stretchers, each one carried by two prisoners. The bodies must have been light. The stretchers, led by the Polish guards, were carried towards the corpse cart. I was so afraid that one of them was Esther.

"At the end of the day, they did another *Appell* to count us. Suddenly I heard someone shout, 'Lily, come here!' It was

Rost and his enormous dog, Ziggy. I went to him on trembling legs and Ziggy licked my hands. Rost took a piece of meat and three slices of bread from a bag and gave them to me. '*Gib es auch deiner Mutter,*' he said (Give some to your mother too). I took the bag and thanked him.

"When I got back to my place in the *Appell*, I scanned all the girls in Schmidts' group. Three were missing, one of whom was Esther."

9

Tom felt Dingo's absence acutely. It felt like a hole in his soul, as if part of him had been taken away. He missed their walks along the Yarkon River, chasing the crows and waterfowl, even Dingo's breath as he lay on his side in Tom's room, his closed eyes opening from time to time, checking that Tom was still there, doing his homework or talking to a friend. At least every day that passed brought Dingo's release date closer. When Tom brought him to quarantine, he had asked the manager, an older man named Eli, if he could come and visit his dog during his stay but Eli had been clear, "Absolutely not. It will be bad for both you and your dog." Meanwhile, the date of the anti-deportation demonstration got closer and Tom and his classmates who planned to join the protest made signs and posters with big pictures of Mikel and his mom. During the lunch break at school, they worked cutting and pasting pictures on signs with slogans like, "Say NO to the deportation of children!" and "Stop the deportation of Mikel." Tom's enthusiasm was infectious and even some kids who were indifferent at first seemed to become interested when they heard about the incident at the bus stop, when the bullies had attacked Tom and Mikel. It was encouraging to see that in spite of everything, there were many people who were unwilling to accept xenophobia and wanted to help. It's easy to demonstrate, thought Tom bitterly, but let's see them hide one of these kids in their own homes.

While Tom's friends were eager to join the effort, most of the students didn't care that much. The students that infuriated Tom the most were those who seemed bothered by foreigners and asylum-seekers. Towards the end of the break one day, Tom went outside to the playground and ran right into Kobi, who had been among the bullies that attacked him and Mikel. Kobi was joking with his group of friends and pointing at Tom who was alone just then.

"Look at this little shit," Kobi said to his friends who laughed along with him. "This guy goes around with that Filipino who's getting deported."

One of his friends happily added, "Great, get them out of here already, I don't like seeing those foreigners contaminating our country!"

The third chastised them, "Really, guys, don't talk like that, they're people just like us. It's not politically correct, right David?"

But David said, "They might be like us but they're ruining our country. Look at the south of the city, it's all foreigners."

Tom felt like he was about to explode. "Kobi, everyone already knows you're racist. You should be ashamed of yourself!"

"Look who should be ashamed. You're the one hanging out with foreigners. That's the real shame!" said Kobi.

"Your behavior is a disgrace to the Jewish people," said Tom, "you remind me of the Hitler youth, the ones who attacked Jews before the war."

"Did you just compare me to Hitler?" Kobi approached him threateningly.

"Yes, like the Hitler youth. You and your crew, too."

"Say it again and I'll knock you out!" Said Kobi.

"I say what I think," Tom dared, and Kobi gave him a powerful push which almost knocked him down. He regained his balance and stood calmly before Kobi, who was bigger than him.

"Get out of my sight, you little traitor," Kobi said, towering over him threateningly.

This time Tom didn't back down. When Kobi raised his hand, Tom grabbed it hard, turned it backwards, and forced Kobi away. With his other hand, he pushed him back and released his grip. Kobi lost his balance and toppled over, breaking his fall with his arm. He let out a cry of pain and lay on the ground squirming. "My hand, my hand, help me!"

But instead of helping him, Kobi's friend started hitting Tom with his fists. Meanwhile, other kids who were nearby came to help Tom and tried to separate him from Kobi's friend. The school nurse ran over. Then came Gilad, the robotics teacher, who took Tom aside, and Ehud, the gym teacher who pulled Kobi's friend away. Luckily, the nurse declared that Kobi's arm wasn't broken, just sprained.

When they sat down in the principal's office, things looked different. There were witnesses who supported Tom, but others who testified against him, saying that he started the fight. Mr. Carmeli, the principal, was angry and ordered both Tom and Kobi to stay off school grounds for a week. Kobi's two friends, David and Elimelach, were each given a warning. Tom tried telling Mr. Carmeli about the attack at the bus stop a week earlier, but it didn't help.

"There will be absolutely no fighting on school grounds," the principal scolded them.

Tom returned home, and Eleanor was surprised to see him back so early. She asked if robotics had been canceled but then she noticed his torn shirt and realized that something bad must have happened at school. Tom knew he couldn't hide his suspension from his parents, especially since the principal gave him a letter asking them to come in for a meeting, so he told her what had happened.

"Oh my God, Tom. Now it's suspension from school! I am very worried," said Eleanor when she sat on the chair by the table, holding her head in her hands for a few seconds. "You are a teen already, a youth even, and it's hard for me to see you getting into trouble like this. Believe me, I know that you aren't guilty here, I trust you. But this is the second time this has happened recently and this time it's serious." When she saw that Tom was on the verge of tears, she went over and stroked his head. "Sweetheart, you will always be my beloved son, don't think for a moment that I'm mad at you or don't love you." She kissed his forehead. "I'm just worried about you, Tom. I hope that this suspension won't affect your future at school. Meanwhile, you can keep up with your schoolwork at home. It's not the end of the world. There have been times in the past when kids studied at home," she added. "And we'll help you, don't worry."

She brought him a snack and sat looking at him sadly. "You probably think that I'm a terrible mother," she said. "But just so you know, my life back in Philly wasn't easy either. My parents were very wealthy, which made all my friends keep their distance. I remember when the girls in my class excluded me in Junior High," she recalled. "And the worst was that Jennifer, the most popular girl in the class, hated me. They called me a snob, maybe because of the home I came from. But I just wanted friends so badly, you have no idea," Tom saw her eyes moisten.

"You know how I don't love birthdays?" She asked.

Tom nodded his head and said, "You always celebrate *my* birthdays, but not yours."

"On my thirteenth birthday, my mother made a big effort, planning a party with a magician and treats for each girl. We made beautiful invitations that I gave to everyone and on the day of the party, we hung balloons over the gate to the garden and all along the path. I wore a new dress that my mother bought me, but apart from the magician, nobody showed up. I will never forget the bitter disappointment I felt that day. In a way, it still hurts. Obviously, I didn't talk to any of the girls after that and my parents, who were concerned, transferred me to a private Jewish school in a different neighborhood in the middle of the year." "Wow, Mom, that's terrible! How could they have been so mean?" Tom was shocked. "And how have you not told me that story until now?"

"There are still some things you don't know," said Eleanor, getting up from her seat and standing beside him. "But it's almost four and I should get you to basketball."

"At least I still have that," said Tom as he took his plate to the sink. "They took school away from me," he added sadly. "But that doesn't compare to your sad birthday story."

"You'll have to get used to being home alone all day for the whole week," she said as they got into the car.

"At least Dingo's quarantine ends tomorrow, finally," Tom said happily. "I'll go with Dad to get him tomorrow morning. And then I won't be completely alone."

Towards evening, when he ran into Yula on the bench beside the building again, he didn't tell her about his suspension from school. She asked him if he was sad because of Dingo.

"He comes home tomorrow," said Tom. "It was probably really hard for him there."

"It's still not the end of the world. It's so hard to explain to today's generation what we went through there. For me, at the camp, that really was the end of the world. Remember what I started reading to you?"

"Yes, of course," said Tom excitedly. "I have more time today and I'd be happy to hear more of your memories," he said, turning on the recording application.

"The biggest fear at the camp was not to show up to work.

It was especially important not to be sick. Anyone that got sick and didn't go to work was taken and shot, or "fired" as they said, that same day or the next morning. During *Appell*, everyone was always tense, worried who would be taken this time. It was enough just to look sick, or struggle to stand on your feet, and the chances that they would take you away grew. Those gaunt men, practically ghosts, would suddenly jump on the spot or try to run just to show the overseers that they were in good shape. The men had a harder time standing the mental anguish and working on their feet all day. They were the first victims. The women actually held out longer. It was very hard work that required a lot of patience and precision. The men that couldn't stand it would be beaten to death by the Polish guards.

"In winter, the ground was frozen. Just walking across the snow for nearly an hour was indescribable torture, especially when you didn't have shoes to protect your feet. The shoemakers from a different department would make wooden clogs that were in high demand. Prisoners were eager to buy them in exchange for a little money or a slice of bread.

"But those clogs would fall off during our long walk so, for some time, I kept an eye on a pile of discarded straps that had been used on the wheels of the factory machines. I heard that some girls had already taken some to tie the wooden clogs to their feet. The punishment for taking anything, even an item of clothing or a potato, could be very harsh. But we had to do something to make the walk easier. So I eventually took two straps, one for me and one for Mom, and I hid them underneath my rags. The whole way, I was terrified that one of the guards would find out. On the way back, they would always shout at us, warning: "Anyone caught taking something from the factory will be severely punished." When we finally got back to the barracks without incident, I breathed a sigh of relief.

"We were so afraid of what would happen if we didn't go out to work that we would push ourselves when we were sick, beyond what seemed possible. Sabina told me how one morning she woke up with such terrible stomach pain that she could not get up for work. Her sister, who had promised to look after her, dragged her to work with her with all her strength. But Sabina's condition grew so bad that she couldn't walk and it turned out she had contracted typhoid fever, like many in the camp. 'But a miracle happened,' said Sabina, 'I don't know why, but instead of shooting me, they came and took me to the infirmary.' She told how frightened she had been when they came for her; she had been convinced that this was the end. 'I couldn't believe it when I saw the supervisor with two nurses and a stretcher.'

Yula paused. "You shouldn't worry about Dingo," she said. "He's in good hands. I know, because two dogs of mine went through quarantine," she comforted Tom. Then she resumed her story of the camp infirmary. "At that time, the infirmary really tried to cure people. When it was first established, the two barracks that made up the infirmary served as another elimination arm of the camp. They would let patients just slowly die, and it was still more efficient and cleaner than the firing squad wall. Very sick patients lay on bunks without mattresses or blankets and as their conditions worsened, they would be given deadly injections to speed up the process and make space for more. The cart of corpses, harnessed to two horses, took bodies from the infirmary to the forest to be burned twice a day. Only later, when there weren't enough prisoners and more working hands were needed, did they have the team of doctors, managed by Dr. Handel, give actual medical care. Since marrying Mrs. Markovicova's niece, Dr. Handel, that same medical student and son of the Lviv professor who had nearly been put to death for the grenade sabotage, had been made the camp doctor. Remember that story?" Yula asked Tom but did not wait for his reply. "When Markovicova, with her boots and whip, intervened and saved him at the last minute? There was already a rumor circulating the camp then that she had an eye on him as a match for her niece, Relia.

"Their wedding took place on a snowy winter day in the Feldman family barracks beside the 'white house' of Commandant Markovicova. Relia's father, the merchant Feldman, who Mrs. Markovicova had made responsible for camp provisions, was a crude and stingy man. He held the keys to the food warehouse and everyone hated him and called him 'the fat merchant.'

"All of the white house servants, workers, supervisors, overseers, and managers were invited to the ceremony. The next day, Handel was declared Dr. Handel, the camp physician.

"And then Mom got sick. They didn't take her to the infirmary like Sabina. Dr. Handel's subordinate didn't do his job properly. At first, she was so weak she could barely manage the morning march to the factory. Capo Lolek, who was fond of Mom and always walked beside her, tried to hurry her along, afraid that the Germans would deem her unfit for work. He said he would speak with Sharata to see if she could rest the following day.

"Mom's weakness was probably the result of hunger. For several days in a row, we had barely received our meager portion of food. From our usual two slices of bread at noon, they had gone down to one slice with a spoonful of soup which, during these cold winter days, wasn't even warm. At first, I slipped Mom some of mine without her seeing, because otherwise she would not have accepted it. But one morning she told me, 'I don't think I can walk to the factory today. Yula, I'm so weak.'

"I was terribly frightened. On the one hand, it was important that she rest and get better, so as not to die of exhaustion. On the other hand, to stay behind at the barracks was practically a death sentence. And what if Lolek hadn't spoken to Sharata? Or if Sharata was unmoved and wouldn't let her stay behind? By some miracle, I managed to help her walk. I supported her the entire way to the factory, with Lolek's help. But during work, midday, she suddenly collapsed beside her machine.

"I was terrified that it was the end of her, but then Schmidts, who had a soft spot for her, came, and instead of instructing that she be taken away to the place from which nobody returns, he told the guards to call for a stretcher and take her back to the barracks. I stayed until the end of the shift, of course, and when I returned that evening she was lying exhausted on her bunk. I went to Dr. Handel, sure that he would help with some medicine or a shot but he recommended one of the new doctors who had come on the last transport. When the doctor said he would only be willing to treat my mother in exchange for money, I was shocked. I had nothing to give him, and although he had the glucose and shots that would have saved her, he refused. I will never forget it.

"Mom held out for two more days. She was bloated with hunger and I couldn't do a thing to help her. On her final day, she whispered to me, 'Here, Yulinka, take this, soon I will be leaving this place. Take these,' she said and handed me a little bag with two sugar cubes that was tied to the inside of the rag she wore. 'Take my sugar cubes,' she whispered in Polish, almost silently, 'it will no longer help me. But you might need it some time.' I reached out to her, took her thin hand in mine, and held her tight. I felt her fingers, which were holding mine, slowly let go. A few minutes later she was dead.

"I lay by her side and wept. I cried hard, I cried for my lost youth, my mother's miserable life, and the way in which it ended. The tears flowed from me like water. Then the girls from my barracks, who had always excluded me, came and comforted me in Polish. Not Yiddish.

"I went and sat outside. It was cold but I didn't care. The tears continued to stream down my face as I thought of my poor, pampered mother, who had once had a servant so as not to strain herself with housework. Mom, who loved dressing up to go out in the evening or host guests at the house. I thought about our lives since the Germans invaded. I thought of Dad, too, and was glad that he didn't have to see us suffer like this. There was a cold wind blowing but suddenly I felt hot breath on me. I turned my head and saw Ziggy's big head resting on my legs as if he was sad too and joining me in mourning my mother."

10

Tom was a bit upset about being thrown out of school like that but his friends from class, who came to visit him at home after the suspension, thought he was lucky. They came over whenever they could to cheer him up.

He was distressed by the injustice of the punishment and the feeling that none of his friends had come to his defense. His close friends *had* reported what they had seen on the playground as well as the incident from two weeks earlier, off school property, but nobody could prove that Kobi had been involved in that, and anyway, it was one person's word against the other, so Tom had to pay the price.

The day after Tom was suspended, he and his father went to the quarantine location to pick up Dingo. As soon as they entered the building, they heard dogs yowling, locked inside their cages. Tom, his heart pounding with compassion for them, ran straight toward the dogs, looking for Dingo.

"Why are you running, boy?" Shouted Eli, the manager of the place, who he had met ten days earlier. "You have to come through the office," he told Reuben. But Tom, who was so excited to see Dingo again, told him as he ran, "I have to see him first, I have to!"

As he approached the cage, Dingo recognized Tom and immediately stood up on his hind legs and leaped at the cage door, barking loudly and jumping so forcefully that the cage inched across the floor. He could hardly wait for Eli to open the cage. He burst out and reached his front paws to Tom's shoulders, licking his face excitedly.

"He's very attached to you," Eli told Tom, "I could see it when you dropped him off last week, too."

"How did he manage the quarantine?" Tom asked.

"He really missed you. He whined a lot for the first three days. But eventually, he calmed down... or else exhausted himself," said Eli.

"And did you give him his favorite treats? The ones I left you to give him?" Tom asked.

"Yes, but it only helped for maybe fifteen minutes, at best. He would finish chewing on one and then start whining again," said Eli as they headed toward the office. Tom held tight to Dingo's leash. Back with his owner, he had calmed down somewhat.

"I'll get the forms," Eli told Reuben. "You can sign here, on your way out."

With Dingo home, they resumed their walks on the path along the southern side of the Yarkon River and Tom's mood began to improve.

When Tom's classmates came to visit and brought their note-books with the homework he needed, Tom wondered if maybe something good would come out of this suspension after all? The most exciting was the day after his suspension, when Efrat, the top student in the class, who always got the best grades in every subject including honors math, came by. Efrat was a tall, thin girl with pale skin and freckles all over her face, and particularly across her small nose. She had a space between her two front teeth, which did not detract from her beauty but instead made her beauty unique.

Efrat was always talking about social issues. She was sharp-tongued and knew how to stand her ground. She lived nearby to Tom and once, at the beginning of the year, Tom even walked her home. He really wanted her to be his girlfriend but he was too shy to ask her out, and then basketball started up, with regular practices after school, and he met Mikel. Efrat was busy, too. Apart from cello lessons at the conservatory, she was also on the swim team at the community center.

Whenever she saw him she smiled, and when Tom had mentioned participating in the demonstration for Mikel and the other children of immigrants, she took an active part in the preparations. Now, when she came to visit him, she said, "Tom, you're something else. You know that, right? I knew you were special since the first time we met." She added, "That was even before Mikel, when you had just arrived and everyone called you the weird ginger from the country, we didn't know where. Now, everyone knows who you are and how much you want to help the immigrants' kids. Not everyone would do that." When he told her about his parents' reaction to his idea that Mikel hide out with them in their apartment, she said that her parents would almost certainly have responded the same way. Her mother was very socially active and went to demonstrations about important problems, she said, but she probably wouldn't want to take them home with her, literally.

"I'm not judging her," Efrat said. "She works hard and still manages to be active in all kinds of issues, and support me and my sister on her own since my dad left." When Tom heard that Efrat's parents were divorced, he wondered if it were possible that his parents might separate too, and how he would feel if they did, but the idea felt absurd to him.

"Not that my dad is so involved," said Tom. "But when we were in the country, my mom felt really dependent. She's the one who wanted to move to the city."

"Not my family. My mom is super independent. She is a journalist for 'Maariv,' maybe you've heard of it? Everyone says I'm so my mother's daughter, but I don't see it."

Dingo came along and began to sniff around. Ever since quarantine, he was clingier than usual. He went over to Tom and lay down beside him, resting his head on both paws.

"He's indifferent to me. What do you think that means?"

"I have a theory about dogs and humans, but it's too complicated," said Tom as he petted Dingo behind the ears.

"Oh, I forgot to introduce you. Dingo — Efrat." Tom made a gesture of introduction. "About what you were saying a minute ago, that you're like your mom… I don't know her, but if she's a journalist, maybe whoever thinks you're like her is right. You are smart and knowledgeable and able to demonstrate it," said Tom. "Is that from books? Or newspapers?"

"Both. I've always been interested in what's going on. Tell me, how is it living in the country. Do you miss it?"

"A lot of the time, yeah. At first, I was really mad at my parents for bringing me to the city. And a little apartment on the fourth floor, no less," Tom complained. "I don't have the kind of space I had there, the freedom to run around in the open air…"

Dingo suddenly rose and began to bark. Efrat was surprised and jumped up from the couch where she was sitting. Tom assured her, "He's just announcing that it's time for his walk. Do you want to take a stroll with us or do you have to be somewhere?"

"I can't today," Efrat shrugged, "my mom is coming to pick me up any minute."

"Too bad," said Tom. "It's a nice area to walk in, and Dingo always finds surprises."

"Another time," said Efrat. "Meanwhile, I'll leave you my notebook with the homework. I don't need it until tomorrow. If you want, I'll come again tomorrow after school and we can do the math problems together, and then maybe we can take Dingo for a walk." After Efrat left, Tom decided to visit Yula. This time, a woman who Yula introduced as her daughter came to the door. "Anat, this is Tom. Anat just got back from abroad two days ago," she said from her armchair. "Tom is the young man who lives downstairs; I told you about him. He likes listening to my stories and memories from the camp. Amazing, no?"

Anat had clearly heard about the boy from downstairs on more than one occasion. "Yes," she turned to Tom. "Nice to meet you. Amos told me good things about you too, but it actually all started when your dog knocked Mom over, no?"

"Yeah," said Tom. "But I went to visit her when she was at the hospital and then after in the recovery unit."

"Wouldn't you find it more interesting to play soccer than listen to my mother's stories?"

"First of all, I'm more of a basketball guy than a soccer player, and I actually play regularly with a professional coach."

Later, when Tom told Yula and Anat about what had happened at school and the bullies who talked about our society being contaminated by foreigners, and also that Mikel had been brave enough to come visit that morning, they were taken aback.

"How can that be?" Anat wondered. "That's outright injustice. Instead of just suspending the bully, they're punishing the victim too." Tom also told them about his visit to Mikel's hiding place. "How can Mikel be forced to hide in such a small apartment?" Tom exclaimed. "And with so many other people, all crowded in there like that?"

Yula interrupted the conversation and asked Anat, "Did I tell you and Amos about the time Mom, Aunt Anya, and I hid in the leather drums?"

"I don't remember that one," said Anat. "Tell us so Tom can hear it too."

"Ready and willing," said Tom, "just, with your permission, I'll record it, okay?"

Yula and Anat agreed and Yula began to tell her story:

"It was in the days before the first Great Aktion,[2] in the summer of 1942. We were living on Niska Street then, at the house of my uncle Yulek the tanner and his wife Anya. Anya was a certified bookkeeper at the factory and Yulek managed one of the departments there. You wouldn't believe how we hid. My uncle had these enormous drums in the yard which they used to stretch the hides while they dried. Oh-ho were they stinky! God help us, it stank to high heavens. And we would hide inside those smelly drums all day. From the morning, when my aunt and uncle went to work at the leather factory, until evening."

"And at night?" Tom asked, "Was there room for all of you?"

"At night, I no longer remember how, but we managed. All of us crowded into one little room."

"Who was hiding with you? What about Grandma? Was it after Grandpa was killed?" Anat asked.

"Yes. Grandpa was murdered in April of 1942 and the Aktion was in July of that same year. My grandmother and grandfather and little Felusha were there, too. Now, it's hard to imagine all of us crowding in there together."

"And how did it end?" Anat asked.

"Terribly. One morning we were getting ready to go hide in the drums for the whole day. Yulek and his wife had already

---

2   A Nazi operation involving the assembling and shooting or deporting of Jews to labor or death camps.

gone to work. Suddenly, my cousin Avrasha turned up. He was
pale with fear. Didn't say a word. Evidently, he had seen what
was going on outside. Within a moment the Germans were
inside and led us to the *Umschlagplatz*[3]. At first, we waited for
hours in the street, which was a street paved with big round
stones the size of cats' heads. We were forced to kneel, which
lasted an eternity, and the whole time those stones were press-
ing into our knees until the pain was unbearable and in the
background, we heard the constant screams of mothers being
separated from their babies. When they finally let us stand,
they used their guns to push us into the square and I screamed
hysterically, shamelessly. Grandma couldn't stand my screaming and said something that I will never forget for the rest of
my life: 'even in the face of death, one might do it with dignity.'
She was so angry at me that she took little Felusha by the hand
and pushed ahead to the front of the line. What was she thinking? That she would get something good there? A better spot?
Where was she hurrying with Felusha? We never saw them
again and I felt guilty that my screaming forced them away.
Mom and I searched for them for a long time and didn't find
them. Then suddenly, I saw my best friend Barbara, from the
building, who was also standing in the long selection lineup. I
remember being surprised that they were taking the non-Jews,
too. Poles from noble, Polish families. I really wanted to speak
with her, to ask her how she had come to be here, too, but I

---

3   The holding area by the railway station where Jews were round-
     ed up for deportation.

saw her grim face and didn't want to cause her further pain. I went on looking for my grandmother but she must have been taken by then, along with Felusha, to the place from which nobody returns.

Grandpa was no longer with us either so from then on it was just Mom and me until her end, and always, just like in that Aktion and other unthinkable situations, I always remembered that old Gypsy woman's promise to me that I would live until ninety-three. Only then would I stop feeling afraid."

She stopped speaking and said, "That's all, I don't have it in me to recall any more terrible things. Tell me something, Tom. You can turn off the recorder now. That's enough." Tom decided to tell her about Gilad. "Actually, I do have something to tell you, something I wasn't sure would interest you, so I didn't mention it until now."

"If you thought it might interest me, why didn't you tell me?" She asked. "You know me by now. I'm still interested and curious despite my advanced age, no?"

"Yes," said Tom. "This time it's about my robotics teacher from school."

"What? You learn robotics in school?" Anat was surprised. "In my days there was no such subject."

"You see, Tom?" Said Yula. "Even Anat is surprised!"

"Not every school has robotics but some of them, like ours, receive funding for enrichment programs. We were lucky to get support from an organization called 'First,' an American organization which is trying to expand awareness of the field among youth."

"Okay, so what are you getting at?" Yula prodded.

"Anyway, my teacher wants to meet you."

"Me? Why would he want to meet me? What interest could he have in me?"

"It all started with the picric acid that you told me about. I wanted to know what it was exactly and nobody was able to explain. Even Google didn't offer any useful information so I asked Gilad, my teacher — or rather, the head of the robotics project — and he was shocked by the question. When he got over his initial surprise, he asked me, 'why picric acid? How did you come to be curious about that? These days it is no longer used as an explosive, it's very dangerous.' When I told him that I knew a Holocaust survivor who was telling me her story about a cruel work camp, he immediately jumped and said, 'it must be Skarzysko-Kamienna.'"

"Ah, really?" Yula was surprised. "How old is he? If he's your teacher he must not have been there."

"That's right. He's too young to have been there. But he might have been there more recently?"

"Nonsense," said Yula dismissively. "Nobody knows where it's located apart from those who were there, maybe their family members, and a few researchers. When people go to that cursed region, they always visit Auschwitz and Majdanek. My cousin, who visited Majdanek not long ago, said that he was there, at Skarzysko-Kamienna."

"Anyway," Tom went on, ignoring Yula's dismissive tone, "he hinted that he was there more recently, under different circumstances, and once he heard about the events that took place at that camp, he had to meet someone who was there. It was hard to digest and believe the things he had heard. He asked me to arrange a meeting with you, if you are willing, and if possible, soon."

11

With his week of school suspension not yet over, staying home and having friends come to visit had begun to feel practically normal for Tom. Most of his classmates were encouraging, but his parents were still angry and felt certain that he was hiding something from them. Reuben, Tom's father, was asked to come to the school to hear about the fight with Kobi, and as much as Tom tried to present the story otherwise, his father was convinced that he had been trying to get revenge on the bully who had attacked him.

"You must understand, Tom, getting into a fight like that is dangerous," he said exasperated. "You don't know what kind of bad people are out there in the world. The fight could have ended differently, if he'd had a knife, for instance." Late in the morning, Mikel came by to visit. In recent days, there had been rumors of immigration inspectors carrying out extensive searches, so Mikel was nervous about leaving the apartment where he was hiding. He had decided to take the risk today after hearing of Tom's suspension. Tom assured him that everyone in the class was looking after him, being supportive and bringing him homework. Mikel told Tom about how challenging the situation was where he was living. His mother was on the verge of collapse, but her friends helped her and gave her strength. There were two other children of immigrants there too and they were all getting ready for the demonstration the following Thursday. Tom showed him the words to the song "I have no other land," which he planned for all the young people to sing together at the protest. He downloaded the song onto his phone and the two listened to it together and tried to sing along with the tune. Evidently, Mikel had a good sense of rhythm and picked it up quickly.

"Do you want to go practice shooting some hoops?" Tom asked Mikel. "There's a court just outside my school, not far from here. What do you say?" Tom tried to convince his friend. "We haven't trained, just the two of us, for a long time."

"You know I would love to go outside," Mikel said sadly. But I'm afraid to walk around too much. Coming here was dangerous enough as it is, with police cars all over the place," Mikel added, getting up from his seat. "It all feels scary. But right now both of us are hanging out at home, not at school," Mikel smiled. "How do you feel about that?"

"It feels insensitive of me to say so," said Tom, "but there have also been some pleasant surprises."

"Like what?" Mikel asked, curious.

"Yesterday Efrat, who I wanted to be my girlfriend, was here. She just turned up to visit me."

"That really is a fun surprise," said Mikel. "That's not my

experience at all, I'm not getting any visits like that," he added sadly.

"What, don't I count?" Tom asked, pretending to be offended. "Did you forget that I came over a week ago?"

"Right," Mikel recalled. "And you were shocked by the decrepit hole we were living in, me and Mom, and her friend and two sons."

"Right," said Tom. "It was a shock for me," he recalled, and only then did he understand how misplaced it had been to complain to his parents about the place they had taken him to, living in a little apartment, several stories high. "When I saw how you were all hiding there, I understood that I live in a palace." Before parting ways, Tom printed out the words to the song that they sang earlier and gave them to Mikel. He asked him to practice it along with his friends. "That way we can all sing it together at the demonstration," Tom said as they got to the bus station where they parted ways with a friendly pat on the shoulder.

That afternoon, Efrat came to visit again. She said that her mother would come at five-thirty to take her to swimming practice.

They went over all of the hard math problems that might be on the next test on extreme functions in differential calculus. Efrat, who was a rigorous teacher and had an excellent grasp of the material, did not skip a single problem. When they finished their homework, she even agreed to take Dingo out together, but not before Tom promised that they would get back on time.

Tom thought that Efrat was different from the other girls in class. She was more straightforward than them and said what she thought. She loved music but didn't care much about all the YouTube stars, the ones that all the other girls went wild for. She also read fantasy and sci-fi books, and he enjoyed talking to her about them, even if Tom thought that the adventures described were too fantastical. Efrat loved the imaginative stories and was sure that at this very moment, as they were speaking to one another, there may well be a parallel universe right beside them that only the lucky few could perceive. She claimed that these books were more than fairy tales and legends. She talked passionately about literature and wanted to introduce Tom to it, too.

Dingo, who had been walking beside Tom all the while, suddenly turned his head and flared his nostrils as they neared the river. "He always sniffs around like crazy right here, as if there's something special in the air," said Tom. "Do you sense something?"

"I don't notice any difference," she said. "And what about you, Tom?" She asked, interested. "You haven't told me what kind of books you like yet."

"Have you read 'The Wisdom of the Pretzel'?" He asked.

"Of course, and I loved it; the second one too, 'King of Hummus and Queen of Bathtub.' I read that one too," said Efrat and then told him about her mother's reaction when she found this book on her desk. "I can't believe that my daughter is reading this sort of thing!" said Efrat, trying to imitate her mother. "That's how she said it while she looked at the book with disgust. She was really shocked. 'I read the reviews of it; it really borders on pornography.' She was horrified."

"I thought your mom was more open and modern." Said Tom. "That was the impression you gave me."

"Yeah. You think I wasn't surprised by her response? I told her that this was ultimately just a book that describes the search for real love in contemporary language. You should read it," she told Tom enthusiastically. "I enjoyed the descriptions so much, and the writer's subtle observations about the lives of youth in Tel Aviv today. Highly recommended."

Dingo suddenly lay down on the dirt like he was lying in wait. Tom and Efrat stopped and saw reeds trembling for a moment, when two partridges emerged, running across the path, and Dingo leaped toward them.

"Did you see that?" Tom asked. "He has sharp senses. Just like a hunting dog."

"What are those birds that flew away? They looked like chickens," said Efrat.

"They are from the same family actually," Tom explained. "Those are partridges. Do you ever watch National Geographic programs?"

"Sometimes. But I usually watch shows," said Efrat and began telling Tom about a TV series she liked, and boasted that she could quote whole dialogues from Sponge Bob.

Then she told him that she kept a journal. She started writing when her parents got divorced. She would go to Tamar the psychologist, who helped her to get through the crisis. Tamar suggested she write about what she was going through every day. She was ten years old then, and when she reads what she wrote then, she is embarrassed by herself.

Her parents went to therapy too, she told Tom, to help them avoid separating, but it was so stupid because they were always fighting. Even in front of her. "If the therapist only knew about just a fraction of their fighting, he would have thrown his hands up way sooner. But what does he care?" Said Efrat. "At least he got his fat check every time. I don't understand why people even get married if they wind up fighting and shouting all the time," she concluded.

"It's just the opposite at my house," said Tom. "They don't shout at all but they don't have much in common. Mom lives in her world and Dad lives in his. I don't understand what they're doing together."

"Maybe they loved each other once and now they're over it," said Efrat. "Like what we learned in physics about the water anomaly. Here the anomaly is you get married because of love, but living together actually ruins that love. No?"

Tom felt a deep affection for this clever girl. She was more than a friend from class and a homework buddy. He felt there were parts of her soul he could understand and he wanted to spend as much time with her as he could.

They kept walking and suddenly Tom noticed her hand was holding his. It had happened so naturally, that he almost hadn't noticed.

"Are you sure we'll make it back in time?" She asked.

"I know a shortcut," said Tom. "We won't go back the same way we came."

They got home ten minutes early and ran right into Amos walking out to his car.

"Hey Tom, how are you doing?" He asked. "Are you back at school yet? I see that you have nonstop visitors."

Tom smiled. "I go back to school next week. This is Efrat from my class." He pointed to Efrat and said, "Efrat, Amos. He's the son of Yula, the woman I told you about."

"Interesting story you told my mother yesterday," said Amos. "I'm curious what the connection is between your robotics teacher and that camp in Poland."

"Yes, we will find out when he comes to speak with Yula," Tom replied. "I'm really curious too. I will try to check with him if he can come next week."

"Oh, that reminds me, I have something for you," said Amos. "Mom's memory notebook." Amos searched in his bag, pulled out the notebook, and handed it to Tom. "If you are really interested in writing about her, you should have a look at this. She asked me to give it to you."

"Thank you," said Tom, taking the notebook, before noticing Efrat's mom Maya's green car pull up. She stopped beside the sidewalk and waited for them. They slowed down and moved closer to one another as if they were alone in the world. Tom put his arms around Efrat and pulled her into a hug.

"Tomorrow I'll bring you that book we talked about," she whispered into his ear as he hugged her.

"What's the whispering about?" Maya asked her, standing by the car door, "I see you two don't want to go your separate ways," she added as Tom opened the door like a gentleman, and Efrat got in. As the car drove off, Tom stood on the sidewalk, waving goodbye. Then he went back to the building and instead of taking the elevator, he found himself skipping up the stairs, two, three at a time, practically keeping up with Dingo, who was two steps ahead of him.

At home, his father had not yet returned from work and his mother, who didn't even turn her head from the TV show she was watching, waved to him with her hand and muttered something about preparing dinner soon. Tom went to his room, turned on the light, and sat on the bed. He opened the notebook that Amos had given him, flipped the pages, and read:

After Mom died I felt terribly alone. I cried a lot. All the way to work at the factory, and then at work at the machines. I would cry and the sky cried with me. We would walk in the morning in the rain, slipping on the melting ice. I cried for Mom and for the hard life she had and then for myself who she had left alone in the world because apart from Sabina and Zhota, I didn't have any friends with whom I could share what I was going through.

Zhota explained to me that the Hebrew date on which Mom had died was the 18th of Adar II, the fast of Esther. This didn't mean anything to me because I barely knew the Hebrew months, but Zhota told me that it was significant.

In April, there was talk of a transfer to another camp, again. Ever since we arrived here, in the summer of last year, they were always talking about evacuating the camp or that new people would come. I wish new people would come, I thought, because then we would be the old-timers. We had been here for eight months now but we were still the "newcomers." There's a group of "veterans" who we also call the "Radom people" for the name of the place they came from. We were the Majdanek people and the veterans really abused us at the beginning, calling us spies and thieves, blocking us from using the water taps, not letting us go to the barber. They said we were the worst, that it was a shame to waste so much as a piece of bread on us. There were people who collapsed from the hunger. It's hard to imagine that hatred, and from our own people, hating us just because they arrived at this hell on an earlier transport, and now give themselves privileges.

Also, we were never given clothes. Some of us still had our rags from Majdanek, and some like me had been walking around for months in a "suit" made from paper bags, the packaging paper that the trotyl powder came wrapped in. We shook it out thoroughly until it was clean of dust, then we tied it with string that we scrounged, and ta-da! Clothing! From paper, yes, but it still served to cover our bodies. Later, after I moved to Israel, when they spoke of the death camps, of Auschwitz, and I saw the pictures of people in the camps, I told everyone, "Look, at least they had clothes!" And I pointed at the striped prisoner garb that they wore. We didn't even have that. That was just one difference between our work camp, which was also a death camp, and the other concentration or death camps.

I hadn't taken off my paper suit since I arrived because just taking it off and putting it back on in the morning, with all the strings that needed to be tied, was a process that could take an hour which would be better put toward sleep, which was dearer to me than changing clothes and feeling comfortable.

Ziggy, Rost's dog that everyone was afraid of, knew me in this attire and must have thought it natural to go about like that. He sometimes came to me, bringing a piece of sausage that he held between his teeth, even bags with sugar cubes that must have come from Rost. When Mom was still alive, I would give her the pieces of sausage or sugar cubes and when she asked where I got them, I would tell her that I got them in exchange for something I sold, some object or shoe that I made from cables that I took from the waste pile beside the machines at work.

Food was the thing that occupied us more than anything else, and most of our conversations were about food and how to get our hands on it. At noon in the factory, we would wait for our portion of soup as if it were a delicacy, but we always consumed it with disappointment. It was watery, thin, and with hardly so much as a grain of barley. That was how it was until Professor Ringel came to us, a real math professor from the University of Lodz. The learned professor became a Capo and was responsible for distributing soup to the factory prisoners. He was the one to introduce the "brilliant economic idea," which one of the pikriners called simply: "Taking the last of morsel from the dead."

Ringel's idea was that everyone agree to give him ten grams of their daily bread allotment in exchange for a spoonful of a thicker, higher quality soup. He reasoned that "in any case, most of you will die here in the next couple of months, so at least at the end of the month I will have two loaves of bread." The rumor spread and when it reached the ears of the German shift manager, he made sure to transfer the professor from his role to a picric acid line worker.

After Mom died, and there was increasing talk that they would move us to a different camp, there was an atmosphere of looser discipline. People from the camp braved sabotaging the German war effort and everyone did what they could to sabotage the munitions and explosives, especially by replacing good shells with defective ones. I also tried this, since Mom was no longer with me and I felt more independent. I would move more good ammunition to the schmaltz crate, pour too little explosive material into the shell caps, and place them in the crates of good shells, hoping that they wouldn't be discovered and that maybe there wouldn't even be any reviews of our work.

Someone from Camp B, Sabina's camp, said that she sabotaged the German ammunition by pouring water into the big boilers where the trotyl mix was prepared. Meanwhile, many shells from production halls six and fifty-three were found to be defective. When it was discovered, they blamed the Jewish overseer, Roman Gerstel.

In the Appell that took place the following morning, Rost sicced Ziggy on him, who dragged poor Roman, screaming in pain and fear, to the truck. At the last moment, someone *realized that they couldn't afford to kill him. He was still needed for factory production, which is how Roman Gerstel was saved.*

That month, building projects began at the camp, evidence that they were planning to evacuate us and bring a new transport of workers. So on the one hand, there was a new need for workers for construction, while on the other, the senior officers wanted to refresh the ranks of the picric acid workers, replacing those among them who were no longer effective.

And then a miracle happened. One day there was a visit from the SS Officer's council at the camp, after which we were all called to an urgent Appell. *It wasn't a normal hour for* Appell, *which was itself enough reason to be concerned. We stood in long lines in the cold, some of us in rags and others, like me, wrapped in our paper suits. From afar, I saw Ziggy up ahead and behind him hurried Dr. Rost, joined by the overseers Hecht and Walter. Rost himself carried out the selection. He would stop before each victim in turn, taking a slow step and looking at the shell of a person before him trying to ascertain if it was worth keeping him on to work. Some of the men were jumping on the spot to show that they were still strong and of use, but even that did not necessarily save them. The screams of those chosen echoed terribly, but the cruel trio kept going until they had chosen twenty-nine picric acid workers who would be sent to the place from which nobody returned. But something was amiss. The head doctor of the camp, Dr. Handel, who had been chosen for the role thanks to his marriage to the niece of the*

Commandant, managed to convince the managers, headed by Dr. Rost, that they had lung ailments and would recover and be able to further benefit the urgent building project to prepare the camp for the next wave of prisoners. And maybe their work would be useful in preparing the camp for the next inspection by the high-ranking SS officers as well.

Those pikriners *really were sent to work in construction and the overseer took pity on them and gave them lighter work. But the need for picric acid workers instead of those who were chosen remained, and the next day at* Appell, *twenty-nine other prisoners were chosen to join the picric acid department.*

Tom couldn't bear the terrible memories and he closed the notebook and set it aside.

***

The next day, Friday afternoon, Eviatar from the Roboner team came to visit Tom.

"Don't ask," Eviatar said. "There was no robotics class today and it's canceled next week too."

"Did something happen?" Tom asked with concern.

"Yes. Gilad didn't come to school. The principal told us that he was called abroad on urgent matters. They are saying he went to Poland for some unspecified amount of time."

12

A week passed, and again there was no robotics class. Instead, the students received extra training in the "C" programming language from Lior, the computer programming teacher. Everyone tried to guess where Gilad, the robotics teacher, had disappeared to. And what was the urgency about? Maybe he worked for the Ministry of Defense? Or maybe he was a Mossad agent and working at the school was just a cover? Tom tried to make sense of the hints he had gotten from Gilad during the last class, about the camp in Poland, the one from Yula's stories, and the mysterious disappearance. He did not share the hints with anyone from class. What had troubled Tom since the previous Monday was Mikel's announcement that they were to be deported that Monday evening, even though last week's demonstration had been so successful. Many of both his and Mikel's classmates came. There were speeches about the terrible injustice, and a nation whose history was rife with persecution, and how was it possible that here in Israel youth like Mikel, who had been raised and educated here, could be deported from the place that was their home? There were artists at the protest who sang patriotic songs and students in T-shirts with Mikel's picture on it, waving posters with the caption "Don't deport children." The song that Tom organized for the foreign students and his classmates to sing moved everyone and there was hardly a dry eye in the crowd, especially when the group of kids from Mikel's school in the south of the city sang the song 'One Human Tapestry':

"And if one of us, leaves us, something within us dies, something remains with him."

Reporters filmed, interviews were broadcast, and everything was so successful and well organized that everyone felt sure that the immigration authorities would remove the pressure and let the foreign children stay. Back at home, Tom thanked his parents, who had also shown up to demonstrate. It was a big surprise to Tom since they had not mentioned it once. The next day at school, everyone praised the successful demonstration and Tom's hard work, but on Monday, when Tom was sure he would see Mikel on the basketball court as usual, after they talked on Saturday on the phone and everything sounded fine and hopeful, Tom was surprised that he did not show up to practice. Adrian, the coach, said that he was worried that despite the great demonstration, it might not have changed anything, and he had a bad feeling. A heavy cloud hung over the game that day. Everyone was affected by Adrian's concern.

In the evening, the phone rang. It was Mikel calling to say that immigration officers had been by earlier and given them deportation papers. They had to get on a plane to Manila to-morrow. Tom was stunned. He had believed that the matter was behind them, and now Mikel was telling him that not only was it unsolved, but tomorrow he and his mother were leaving. He tried to encourage Mikel, but it seemed the words coming out of his mouth fell on deaf ears. Mikel was in despair.

"Don't worry, Mikel," Tom said, trying to sound confident. "Tomorrow we will all come to the airport, maybe we can do something."

"It's a lost cause, Tom," said Mikel, sounding hopeless. "We lost, and they won." That night, Tom had trouble falling asleep and decided to arrange for the students to come to the airport with their shirts and posters. And so they did. Everyone came. Some by train and some by bus, the whole basketball team and Adrian himself, too. Everyone wore the red shirts of Hapoel Tel Aviv and stood in the departure hall at eight in the evening, even though the flight to Manila wasn't until eleven. Tom and Eviatar stood beside the gate to let everyone know when they were coming, but there was no sign of Mikel and his mother. Only at the last moment, right before the flight began board-ing, an official-looking vehicle with the immigration emblem on it stopped suddenly beside the entrance gate. A young man with his hood over his head and a short woman stepped out, accompanied by an officer and two young women who turned out to be representatives from the immigration authority. One of them held a file with documents in one hand and with the other she led the youth, his face hidden, toward the entrance hall.

Tom recognized Mikel at once and waved to him. The short woman by his side was his mother Roz, who Tom had met at their apartment and the demonstration. Eviatar ran straight to the group beside the counters to inform them that Mikel was on his way, but the policeman led them through a shortcut without need for inspection, straight to the border control gate, where family members usually said goodbye to travelers.

Everything was done quickly and discretely. By the time Tom's group understood that they were taking Mikel and his mother through the shortcut, they all ran toward the gate, where they waved their posters and began to sing "One Human Tapestry" as tears streamed down their cheeks. Mikel stood at the gate, facing his friends, and must have asked his escorts to let him at least say goodbye. He stood still for a few seconds, waving two fingers in a sign of victory. Then he blew kisses to his friends and was led through the gate. When the reporters arrived, there was no longer anything to photograph apart from the group of students, waving their signs. The interviewer approached Adrian and asked him a few questions, but Adrian didn't talk long, just spoke about Mikel, the wonderful youth who played basketball with him for two years as part of "Basketball for All." A young man beloved by all, who was as Israeli as the rest of his teammates. Both in appearance and language, one could hardly even detect any difference. He also mentioned basketball's amazing capacity to bring people together and connect them, even from remote corners of the world.

On the way home everyone was depressed, nobody had expected the immigration police to move so quickly or smoothly, not allowing for anything more than a quick wave goodbye and a picture for the newspaper. A bitter feeling accompanied Tom for the next few days. He also felt less engaged in his studies. The canceled robotics class with Gilad only added to the dismal feeling. He thought that maybe an outing with Dingo in the park would make him feel a bit better, but it didn't help.

That afternoon, Efrat came over again and they talked a lot about the previous day's events and the evening at the airport. Efrat was also furious about the incident and told Tom that when she told her mother about what had happened to Mikel, her mother had been surprised that she knew nothing of the deportation. Efrat quoted her mother, "Why didn't you tell me anything? Why didn't you share that with me?" Her mother had said. "I could have sent a reporter and photographer, this is good material for a big scoop!"

"You understand, Tom?" She said, her voice shaking. "That's what interests her, her scoop," she added. "What does she want from me? When exactly was I meant to share it with her? After all, I barely see her. She never even has time for me." Tears welled up in Efrat's eyes. "Only at night, before bed and in the morning for a few minutes, when she's drinking coffee and driving me to school. That's the only time we see each other. Ah, and also at swim practice, like now, she's supposed to come pick me up here again. I'm sure that's why Dad left, because she puts all of her time into work and is barely around or interested in the house or family," Efrat said and wiped tears from her eyes.

Tom put an arm around her shoulders and she rested her head on him, taking comfort in his embrace. As Tom walked Efrat out to the curb where her mother was meant to come get her, the two ran into Yula and her caregiver on the bench, and Tom greeted her. Afterward, he said, "Yesterday, I read your notebook that Amos gave me and I couldn't fall asleep afterward. I also read about the sabotage attempts at the camp. It's hard to believe what you went through there."

Yula nodded sadly and said, "Yes, Tom, it is hard to believe. Which is why I write. It should be remembered. Nobody should forget what we went through there."

"It's so important that you write down your memories, to preserve them." Tom placed his hand on Yula's shoulder and told her, "Yula, this is Efrat. She and I are in the same class at school. Efrat met Amos when he gave me your notebook."

Efrat nodded and smiled and said, "Nice to meet you."

"We are waiting for Efrat's mom, who is supposed to come pick her up," said Tom, and the two said goodbye to Yula. As they stood waiting, Efrat asked Tom what they were talking about, so he told her.

"And you didn't mention a word of this to me?" She was surprised.

"I didn't think it would interest you," Tom replied. "It's a notebook of her memories that Yula wrote about the time she was in that camp in Poland. You were there when Amos gave it to me," he said. "And besides, we had lots of other things to do and to talk about, I guess I didn't get around to it."

Just then Maya's green Audi pulled up beside them.

"Do you think she's unhappy about our relationship?" Tom asked as he put his arms around Efrat's shoulders and pulled her into a hug.

"How could you think that?" She whispered in his ear. "Quite the opposite, she actually says good things about you," she whispered and kissed his neck.

"Hey, what are you two talking about?" Maya asked with a smile and opened the car door.

"Just a moment, Mom," said Efrat before getting into the passenger seat. Tom heard the click of her seatbelt and she waved goodbye through the window.

That evening, before bed, Tom continued reading from Yula's notebook:

The frost on the ground was long gone and spring was upon us. The freezing winds no longer pummeled us as we walked to the factory in the morning. Just the shouting of the Jewish Capo and the Polish police hurrying us. The other girls in our barracks were already talking about Passover approaching. That didn't affect me much. Even back home, we hadn't bothered with the Passover seder. I remember two times that we had a seder at my grandmother's home in Favya Street with Mom's parents. They let me read the four questions that we had learned back at the Jewish school and I didn't understand what they were or what they wanted from me.

The work at the factory helped me not think about Mom all the time. I missed her most at night. I was used to her being on the bunk below mine, close to the heater. In the winter it was the best place to escape the terrible cold. The girls were jealous of us for being close to the heater, which was like a meeting place for those who wanted a little company in the evening. So it served not just as a source of heat but also a stove to warm tea or toast bread and even to dry the rags that some of the girls wore and occasionally washed.

Friday evenings always had a different atmosphere in our living quarters. Someone got ahold of a candle, lit it on Friday evening at the edge of the bunk, and covered her face to say the blessings over the Shabbat candles, as we had learned at the Jewish school. At home, Mom hadn't done the Friday evening ritual and Dad didn't recite the Kiddush. Here, there were times when even Mom lit the candle on her bunk and covered her eyes to say the prayer, which I was surprised to hear she had not forgotten. "It helps me remember Dad," she would tell me afterward. Sometimes Dora, who had the most beautiful voice, would sing mournful songs in Yiddish and would receive a cooked potato or a slice of bread.

The coming Wednesday there would be a Passover seder in the barracks for the most orthodox among us. They said that there was an agreement with the Commandant Markovicova herself and that she had even agreed to assign police officers to guard the barracks entrance.

We didn't see Mrs. Markovicova much. Most of the time she was in her office, which the veterans referred to as "the white house." There, surrounded by her trusted assistants, she gave orders and pulled strings concerning everything that happened in the camp, apart from the factory work, for which Dr. Rost and his assistants were responsible. Usually, when we saw her with one of her helpers outside the white house it was a bad sign, and that day was no exception. It was Friday and everyone was expecting a Friday evening atmosphere, usually conducted by some of the girls from the barracks. But before we even returned to the barracks to arrange ourselves on the bunks, the sound of horses broke the silence. It was the cruel bully of a police commander, Eisenberg, who came galloping on his horse, a baton in his hand, in his crisp uniform. He approached the policemen surrounding Mrs. Markovicova and ordered, "Appell in five minutes, everyone out!"

When we stood in Appell before the police chief on his horse and Commandant Markovicova's entourage, we were surprised to see Mr. Feldman, her other brother-in-law, the one in charge of the food stores, at her side. The keys in his hand made a shaking sound. Markovicova had given him the keys to the food warehouse and made him the most hated man in the camp. In charge of supplies.

Nobody knew what was going on and everyone stood shaking with fear and from the cold. She paced back and forth with her whip under her arm, her tall, elegant boots covered in mud. She suddenly raised her voice. "Whoever is responsible for breaking into the food storehouse and stealing the bread, take one step forward!"

Nobody moved. Everyone shook with fear. Most of us did not know about the break-in to the warehouse.

"Bunch of fearful whores. That's what you are," she said and pulled the whip out from under her arm, snapping it in the air until just the sound of the lash hurt without so much as touching me. People here were dying of hunger while in the white house, the house of the crime family, and in the house of the police chief and the merchant Feldman, there was no shortage of food. Around here, prisoners were willing to die for half a slice of bread. Sometimes people showed great compassion to one another, when those who were stronger were able to give their slice of bread to a friend who was starving, so it's a wonder anyone tried to break into fat Feldman's storehouse.

"Whores with no conscience, what do you need that you come stealing at night from everyone's warehouse, from the stores of bread that are meant for all of the prisoners?" She shouted. "Aren't you ashamed?"

All the while Eisenberg, the police chief, tried to restrain his horse, who was stamping his feet nervously. He was even calm enough to take a pack of cigarettes out of his pocket, pull one out, and light it. After blowing the smoke out into the cold air, he said, "If nobody comes forward in the next two minutes," he raised his voice, "I will decide on the guilty parties myself!" He called over Dr. Rost, who stood nearby with his frightful dog, and whispered to him. Several seconds later, two men took a step forward to admit their guilt. Friends of one of them, Yashak, later explained that he had broken in on behalf of his younger girlfriend who was starving in the picric acid department.

I will not write what happened to Yashak and his friend here.

Then Wednesday came and everyone was talking about the Passover Seder. Not everyone was invited. Eliezer from the picric acid unit took charge and even pleaded with Mrs. Markovicova to let it happen. Maybe the food warehouse incident, and the hysteria all around when Rost's dog did what he did, weighed on her. Maybe her conscience tormented her, thinking of her extravagant white house compared to the lives of the prisoners starving to death. And there were those who said that it was all thanks to Mrs. Gutman, the Commandant's mother, who still observed the Sabbath and was the good Yiddishe Mama of the family. Maybe she pressured her daughter to agree to hold a Passover seder for a few rabbis in the C camp, but those who were there said it had been a very sad Passover seder. With armed Polish officers guarding the entrance, there could be no festive atmosphere. Despite the white paper covering the tables, and despite Mrs. Markovicova's effort, sending a bowl of eggs as a holiday gift, which stood in the center of the table, it was a depressing seder, said Zhota, who had been invited. Instead of wine, they poured borscht into cans which served as cups. In the absence of the Passover Haggadah, they recited verses from memory, with every sentence reminding them of the fate of the slaves in Egypt which was not half as bad as that of the camp inmates. Between one verse and the next, the soft crying of the people gathered was heard.

Zhota understood the heart of Mrs. Gutman, the mother of the family, and told me of the big argument between her and her daughter before Relia, Markovicova's niece's wedding.

"Don't you tell me what's good for Relia," the commandant

shrieked at her mother. "I am responsible here and it breaks my heart to see her alone while everyone around her is married."

Mrs. Guttman was furious, "With all due respect, Commandant, you do not feel that you are hurting others, and you should know," she said, as she wagged her finger at her, "you have ruined our whole family bringing us here to this damned camp. It's lucky your father isn't here to see this performance of yours, with French lessons for your sisters. Who needs French when people around us are starving to death? There isn't so much as a drop of humanity in you!"

Zhota added that she had heard Mrs. Markovicova saying, during that same fight, that soon this nightmare would be over and by summer the people would be transferred to another camp.

At night now, I dream of Mom more than Dad. One night she appeared in my dream in a new dress that she had bought herself with a wrapped gift in a box for me. "Here, Yulinka," she said. "This is for you." I opened the box and inside it was a dress exactly like Mom's. As I was planning to try it on, I realized that I was now wearing a smelly suit made of paper without so much as underwear. The thought of Mom dressed so beautifully, bringing me a present, and me still in the camp paper, woke me from the dream, so I lay in the dark and listened to the breathing of the exhausted women, who had spent the previous day working hard in the factory. Suddenly, from the far side of the barracks, a sharp wail recalled the hysteria of just a few days earlier, when Eisenberg sat comfortably on his horse with *a cigarette emitting blue smoke. The horse stamped its feet nervously, but Eisenberg just sat motionless on the saddle as Dr. Rost's enormous dog raged.*

13

Ever since Mikel was deported to the Philippines, Tom felt less tension at school, but the suffocating anger at the cruel deportation did not leave him. Since his suspension, the boys who had harassed him had let up. Maybe they felt like they had won since, in fact, they seemed to have gotten what they wanted.

While the social tension might have diminished, the pressure at school only grew. In another two weeks was the big history exam and he felt he could scarcely recall the huge amount of material that they had been given. He also had a big math exam coming up, and that was even more of a challenge. His father had already been asked to come to talk to the teacher, Shaul, who Tom actually really liked, and had given Reuben a rather bleak picture. The only good grades Tom was getting were from Gila, the literature teacher, for his expressive abilities and the essay he wrote on the subject of his choosing. She told Reuben that Tom had literary talent worth developing and said how amazed she had been by his last essay. This was the only ray of light for Reuben at that parent-teacher meeting a month earlier.

"Okay, so we have a young author in the house, but that does not get him anywhere if these math grades don't improve," Reuben said to Eleanor at dinner.

"Quit pressuring him like that," said Eleanor. "Not everyone needs math. It's good to get good grades, but you can manage just fine with low grades too. And what does that mean to manage? It's not like he's going straight to university, what's with the pressure?"

"All I know is that he needs his matriculation certificate and without math, that's impossible," Reuben said as he folded the newspaper that he had just been staring at anyway.

"Haven't you noticed that ever since Mikel, his Philippino friend, was deported, he doesn't go to basketball anymore? That worries me even more."

"He started running instead," said Reuben. "I also ran when I was his age, before the army."

"Army? He's not even sixteen yet, for God's sake, what does the army have to do with anything?" Eleanor said and added, "and I intend to make sure he doesn't go into some combat unit. He's our only son."

"Where is he now?" Reuben asked. "He should have been home by seven."

Just then the door opened and Tom and Efrat came in.

"O-ho! Welcome, you're right on time," Reuben cheered. "Come sit with us."

"How are you, Efrat?" Eleanor asked after the two of them

sat down. "How's school going?"

"Fine," said Efrat modestly. "I'm helping Tom get through some math material and Tom is teaching me about canine body language."

"Yes, Tom told us," Eleanor said, smiling. "Are you also thinking of skipping the trip to Poland next year?"

"Why are you involving her?" Tom fumed. "It's my decision," he said and added, "just so you know, the hypocrisy kills me." Now he was truly mad. "If it was up to me I would have canceled the whole unnecessary trip ages ago."

"It seems to me like a very important experience," said Reuben. "It's an excellent way to teach the younger generation about the horrors of that war."

"Please let's not have this argument now, I'm going to make omelets. The salad is already on the table," said Eleanor as she got up from her chair.

But Tom went on. "Maybe it's too soon to say what I think about the matter, but in any case, I'm not going."

"What do you mean?" Asked Reuben, surprised. "If the whole class goes, you'll go too."

"You should be grateful I'm saving you over a thousand dollars…" Tom said to his parents.

"What, is it because of money? What are you talking about? Tom, what's going on with you?" Reuben was angry. "If the whole class goes next year, you'll go with them."

"If everyone were paired with a Holocaust survivor to just listen to his or her story like I'm doing, we could save the whole song and dance of the 'trip to Poland.' Hard to say what it actually teaches at this point," Tom said angrily. "A bunch of excited teenagers traveling in the name of justice, wrapped in flags at an extermination camp that they don't know a thing about, and in the evening, they go to some bar in Krakow or Warsaw, as if they deserve it."

Now he couldn't be stopped. "And another thing, the Holocaust wasn't just Auschwitz and the Warsaw Ghetto. They don't talk about that, about the work camps like Skarzys-ko-Kamienna, where people were worked to death, and if they didn't die from the picric acid fumes, then they were killed in the shooting range. There's nothing for me in Poland, not next year, and certainly not as a part of this hypocritical project."

They could hear the pop of oil from the pan on the stove and the smell of fried eggs wafted into the room. Efrat was surprised by the intensity of Tom's feelings. His blood was boiling with his anger at the whole industry of the trip.

"It's a real industry, and it takes millions from parents who feel helpless and obligated," Tom went on. "Just another Zion-ist duty, to perpetuate the resentment and hatred throughout the generations. Haven't we done enough of that already?"

"Hang on a moment, Tom," said Reuben. "There's no point having this conversation right now," he ruled, and added, "I am the last person to convince you to go against your wishes."

"Now, everyone calm down and give me your plates," Eleanor said, returning with the still-bubbling omelet in the pan. "Take some salad too, it's fresh and tasty," she added, serving some eggs onto Efrat's plate.

"Not so much," said Efrat, stopping Eleanor.

"Now a truce," Tom said with a smile and handed his plate to his mother. "Eat, Efrat," Tom said, "You must be hungry after our long walk."

It really had been a long walk. Whenever Efrat came over they would go for a walk outside in nature. Since he had shown her his favorite spot, the hidden one where he would go to be alone, she too was captivated by its charm. It was a knoll with a shaded bench at the top, from which you could see the place where the two rivers, the Yarkon and Ayalon, intersect, giving it the shape of a bird's head and creating an ideal habitat for a wide variety of birds, which is why the intersection is called Rosh Tzippor ("bird's head"). There was a big bridge for the highway to run over the Ayalon River and the sound of the speeding cars surrounded the whole area. But the knoll was quiet, and Tom would let Dingo off the leash to run around after other dogs while he sat and watched.

Efrat, like him, loved the quiet of the place and the view of the two rivers intersecting. They would sit there holding hands, and enjoy the quiet as the sun went down over the eucalyptus trees.

When they set off for their walk, before going home to Tom's house and getting into the discussion about the trip to Poland, Tom felt a sudden longing for the village of his childhood. He told Efrat that the trees here reminded him very much of the boulevard of Eucalyptus trees where he grew up until they came here to live in the city, at the edge of Ramat Gan, not far from the wild vegetation by the river. Here, there were also tall eucalyptus trees with trunks thick enough that you could carve a heart with an arrow through it. Efrat suggested they do that, and Tom told her how in his childhood, when he carved his name into a tree, the neighbor was so mad at him she told him that trees feel pain too. Efrat thought that the idea sounded so nice and told him, "You're a special guy, Tom, have you heard that before?"

"No," Tom said and smiled in embarrassment, "I've just been told that if my math grades don't improve, I won't be able to stay at this school."

"Nonsense, Tom," she replied. "I promise I'll help you and you'll do great. You'll see." She stroked his hand and he felt chills up his back. Efrat put her arm over his shoulder and gently pulled him to her. The knoll was theirs alone at that moment. Even if anyone else had been there, they wouldn't have noticed. They were lost in one another. She brought his face closer and he felt her smooth lips over his, dry with excitement. He wondered if this is what love feels like.

"This really is the closest thing to love," Efrat said suddenly. Had she read his mind? But at precisely that dreamy moment, Tom noticed Dingo's restrained growl. He had been lying, not far from them, tied by his leash to a post, but now his growl signaled a coming threat and his drooping ears perked up.

"I think Dingo must have sensed some dog nearby," Tom said and stood up, pulling Efrat with him. "We need to be alert now. We don't see anyone yet, but Dingo probably smells him already." He held Efrat's hand as he scanned the lower part of the hill. "There, they're coming towards us," Tom said. "See? Dogs notice things long before we do." Tom's concern was justified. Coming up the hill was a big, black Rottweiler. A slim girl was holding onto his leash, barely able to restrain her dog, who was already on his hind legs, pulling toward Dingo. This was not a dog coming to play. Tom saw Dingo's grim face, shaking his whiskers as if to say, don't come near me. But it didn't help. The black dog leapt and within seconds, the two dogs were rolling on the ground. Dingo, who was lighter and faster, caught the heavy Rottweiler's neck in his jaws as he tried to subdue him. The dog's owner tried with all her might to hold onto the leash, but he got away from her. She looked hysterical. Now Tom was standing beside the two wrestlers and in the most commanding voice that he could muster, cried: "Dingo, stop!" As if by magic, Dingo stopped and raised his head, saliva dripping from his mouth, as red as blood.

"Dingo! Here!" Tom shouted again and pulled the leash which had gotten tangled up with the black dog's leash. "Come here, Dingo!" He turned to him gently now and even though Dingo had not had obedience training with a professional dog trainer, he approached Tom with his head down. Efrat watched it all play out, frozen to her spot, and did not utter a sound. "Call your dog, gently, now, don't shout," Tom instructed the helpless girl, who stood shaking, in sharp contrast to her powerful, aggressive dog. Tom stood patting Dingo gently, took his leash, and turned to Efrat who stood stunned beside him.

"Scared you a little, huh?" He said and took her hand in his. He pulled her to him and hugged her to calm her down. They finished eating dinner and went to Tom's room to prepare for the big math test, which was only two days away. When the door closed behind them, Efrat hugged him and gave him a long kiss on the mouth. Then she told him how proud she was of him for standing up for his beliefs regarding the Poland trip and that she would do the same, though she wasn't as rebellious.

"After reading about everything that happened in that camp in Yula's notebook, I think there's no point in another batch of kids wrapped in flags going to Warsaw of all places, or Auschwitz, as if that was the only place where the Holocaust happened," he said. "And what I am learning, reading Yula's journal and talking to her, is invaluable and more meaningful than any trip or lecture about what happened at the extermination camps. Do I really need some stuffy lecture or someone trying to squeeze tears out of us beside the pile of shoes at the camp?"

Efrat went on stroking his head and looked him in the eye. Then they sat down and began to focus on the exam material, which included everything they had learned until now, including analytical geometry, which Tom also struggled with. Efrat sat with him patiently and did not give up until he solved the problems on his own. And it worked. In a differential calculus test a week ago he had gotten an 88, and a comment from the teacher: "Good progress, keep it up."

Before leaving the room, Tom said, "I have to show you a short piece from Yula's journal. The one that Amos gave me that time. I read it yesterday. Here, you read it, too." He handed her the notebook, open to the intended page:

Everyone is talking excitedly and hopefully about them moving us to a different camp. I'm actually not looking forward to it. The move from Majdanek to here was enough for me, when Mom and I were so grateful to the hangman at Majdanek who did us a favor and transferred us to Skarzysko-Kamienna. From one hell to another, which turned out to be worse.

What is there to be happy about here, with them cleaning the camp so nicely and painting the buildings? It doesn't make me happy, unless it turns out that the next place is better, or I will be sorry, mostly about Mom, who didn't survive this camp and just got thinner and thinner until she practically disappeared. Even before she was sick, she was a skeleton, and I went to great lengths to bring her something to eat. When we would pass through the field of potatoes on the way back from the factory, I would find one that had been left on the ground and take it and hide it in the bag I kept tied around my waist, hidden under my paper clothes. I was terrified of getting caught because anyone caught would be punished or even shot. Just a few days ago, I saw some men step out of line and snatch a few potatoes. Two of them were put to death that evening. But for Mom, it was worth the risk. I won't forget the surprise that awaited me when, one day, when Mom was still alive, Ziggy, Dr. Rost's dog, came holding a piece of salami in his mouth. He came right to me while I was on my way to the tap to rinse myself in the cold water. He lifted his head up so I would see the surprise in his mouth. I took it from him at once and hid it under my clothes and stroked his head lovingly, and praised him in German. I didn't know if this was Rost's way of expressing his sympathy for me, or if the dog

*had snatched the salami of his own initiative, but I didn't care
and I hurried to Mom who was already lying down, swollen
with hunger on her dirty bunk. I took out the salami and with
the help of a tin lid I had saved, I removed the part with Ziggy's
teeth marks and gave her the good part. I cut it into three pieces,
gave her two, and kept one for myself.*

Efrat closed the notebook and said, "What a life. I don't know
if that even is life. Now I can understand your argument about
the Poland trip better. You've fully immersed yourself in these
horrors. Terrible." She looked at her watch and said, "Okay, I
have to hurry, my mom will be here any minute."

Tom accompanied Efrat outside. It was already after 9 PM,
and Amos was just heading to his car after visiting Yula.

"Good evening," he greeted them. "I'm happy to see you
two," he added and patted Tom on the shoulder.

"Listen, your teacher who wanted to meet with my mother
and tell his story, is he back from abroad yet? You told me that
he disappeared suddenly."

"You mean Gilad, my robotics teacher?" Tom asked. "He
isn't exactly a teacher, he's a volunteer educator for the First
program," he said. "But never mind, no he isn't back yet. It's
like he was swallowed up by the earth. There are lots of theo-
ries, each one crazier than the last."

"Well, just so you know, my mom is very curious to meet
him and now his sudden disappearance makes his story even
more interesting. And another thing," Amos remembered.
"She's been talking a lot lately about that dog that saved her,

and she would like to meet another dog of that breed while she's alive, a Great Dane. Remember you promised to bring her one of those? You know, just for one meeting, just to pet that kind of dog and say thank you, as if it were the same one."

That moment a short honk came from the curb. It was Maya in her green Audi, who had come to pick up Efrat.

14

"I'm back from France, now," Gilad began. "They decided that it was important that I be at the Israeli pavilion at Le Bourget, to present our new anti-tank missile, the 'Gil 2.' And on account of the fact that I now have a management role for missile production in all of the places in the world where it is manufactured, they thought I should be there."

"A great honor, surely" said Amos, "But how is that related to the camp where my mother was, Skarzysko-Kamienna?"

"I'll explain," Gilad replied, setting his cup of coffee down on the table for a moment. He appeared to be rooting around in his black bag, then pulled out some photographs.

"Here," he pointed at the picture showing a group of men, all of them in blue windbreakers with employee tags hanging from their zippers, in front of the ruins of a brick building that looked like an old bunker. "This picture that you see was taken at that camp, Skarzysko-Kamienna."

Yula looked like someone who had just been hit by lightning. "That's the bunker that was behind Mrs. Markovicova's white house. Everyone said that's where she would hide when the Russians came. I remember like it was yesterday. And there's the path, the one we walked on every morning and evening, to the factory and back." She didn't believe that the man sitting before her had been to that terrible place, which was forever etched in her memory as hell on earth. And here he was, sitting with her and showing her a picture of himself with a group of Israelis, against the backdrop of the trail that she had once walked twice a day, every day.

The meeting took place in Yula's living room on a Thursday afternoon. Gilad had been back at school on Monday after two weeks of absence, and during the first class with Gilad, Tom passed Yula's invitation along to him to meet at her place. Tom remembered his great excitement at school on the day Gilad returned and all of the guesses about his absence that had grown and picked up speed while he was gone. Gilad's robotics students, who were closer with him, hounded him with questions about his trip. Was it a trip on behalf of the country? Something related to security? Nobody knew. The rumor mill version was that Gilad was connected to the Mossad and that the work at the school was just his cover story.

"I still don't understand what exactly you did at the camp?" Yula asked.

"At the peak of our activity in Poland, we were testing the anti-tank 'Gil' missile to great success, in all kinds of places," said Gilad, pulling out another photo and showing it to Amos, who seemed interested.

"Here is the Gil missile, the version from a few years ago.

See? One soldier holds it and fires. It doesn't need any special device or armored vehicle. Just a soldier or a team and 'Boom!' Brings down a tank." Tom couldn't take his eyes off Gilad's photos, and he was fascinated by his explanation.

"See the four fins at the back? Those help it navigate to its target," Gilad went on.

"And what are those telescopes on the side of the legs?"

"That's the electro-optical navigation system, which is only effective in the daytime, and sends electro-optic waves at the target. Those detectors are homing devices. At night, the system works on infrared waves," he said, then added another little explanation for Tom. "The detector is like the sensor on the Roboner. We can talk about that later, in class. And here's another thing." He pulled out another photograph. "Something from the factory that we visited, even though the missile testing wasn't on the grounds of the camp but in a firing zone far away, I forgot its name."

Yula stared, wide-eyed. "That's our department! 'Werk C.' Here, from here, the third window, see? That's where I would stand and look out at the trees covered in snow in the winter and dream of freedom, of walking alone between the snowy trees, without shells or Germans shouting, holding batons. In the photo, it's all green, but in winter I would stand here, behind the window, and fill up anti-aircraft shells. I can't believe the building is still there. It's all there. Look, even the black tar roof is still there," she said with great excitement. "All of these red brick walls, and here is the heater with the chimney. There's a window just to the right of it. That's where

I worked. I can't believe it."

She had tears in her eyes. "This is why I never wanted to go there, ever since I left Poland. Or to Majdanek."

Amos asked again how they got to that place in particular and Gilad replied, "We felt that we had an excellent product which had been demonstrated successfully dozens if not hundreds of times, and a bid had just been issued by the Polish army to train one of their manufacturers. The Polish company Mesko sits right on the remains of the German HASAG factory. The bid was to produce an anti-tank missile for them. It was the perfect job for us, that is, for our 'Gil' missile, so we sent a proposal, and surprisingly, we got it. The Polish company and military chose us and invited us to come and demonstrate our missile."

"I'm sorry if the pictures are upsetting to you. I didn't think about how you would feel about them," said Gilad. "Nor did I believe that there were survivors from that terrible camp. They told us that everyone who was there was no longer among the living. They died either from overwork or because they were 'fired,' a euphemism for execution — that is, when they took out and shot prisoners who were too weak and ill from work."

"That's what nearly happened to me at the end," said Yula. "When you finish, maybe I will tell you how they nearly fired me."

"I didn't go through the Holocaust, thank God," said Gilad. "But I am a child of survivors, who saw me as their great success here in Israel. They pushed me in my studies and just wanted me to learn a good profession and not be a carpenter like my father. My dad always told me, 'You will be a scientist, you will be an engineer, not a carpenter like me.' And sure enough, as a teenager, I went to ORT Bialik for high school, a high level vocational school, like a preparatory school for the Technion University."

"Did they tell you what they went through in the Holocaust?" asked Anat, Amos's sister.

"They didn't really tell me, they mostly did not want to talk about that time of their lives," said Gilad. "Only here and there they would say, 'what are you complaining about here in Israel? You think it's cold in the winter? You have no idea how cold we were, and we didn't even have food. We were starving to death. For months we barely ate a thing.' That's what they would say if we complained about cold or anything like that," said Gilad. "I was given the responsibility for the deal with the Poles," Gilad went on. "Also the respect that came with it, because the success of the experiment would land us a huge deal, along with respect. But it also felt like a heavy responsibility. I wasn't the only one in the group who was a child of survivors. There were a few others, like one whose parents had been in nearby Kielce during the slaughter that happened there after the war. They said that they would never ever return to Poland, nor would their children.

"In my case, my dad gave his blessing and said, 'You show the Poles who the Jews are. Back then we weren't worth the dirt on their shoes and now we come with pride and teach them a lesson in technology.' And all of that on my narrow shoulders, which must bear the missile soon, to place it on a launch pad and aim it at a target which would explode into a million fiery sparks ... And I, who had already executed probably hundreds of successful launches, always hitting the mark..." Yula's hand moved to his shoulder in an inadvertent gesture of support of the heroic man who sat beside her.

"And I, who always took very precise shots, and I know the missile like the palm of my hand, after all, it was me who named it 'Gil' and headed its development. And now? All of the history of the Jewish people in Europe from the war years lay on my shoulders. I represented my mother and my father, who were so happy when they bought me my first white lab coat for the Technion Institute of Technology, and now I was standing on Polish soil, in a place where every centimeter is soaked with Jewish blood, literally. For real. I was standing there and the missile is aimed at the tank..." Gilad paused briefly.

"So I'm standing there with the missile, aimed at the tank target, which is three hundred meters away, and I felt that I was unfocused. Maybe I was distracted by thoughts of my parents, their generation and mine coming full circle, but I had some kind of tremor and I knew that something would go wrong this time. Of all times for it to not go right. When the countdown began, my nerves rose. The 'enemy tank' was already at the center of the viewfinder, the countdown was about to end, and I tried to focus for the best possible result. When the countdown finished, I pressed the trigger. The eyes of all of the important guests from Mesko and the Polish military followed the missile trajectory and... BOOM! But where were the flames? The ones that indicate the tank was hit and destroyed? Sweat dripped down my back, I was wet all over from anxiety and nerves and the Polish officer who had followed the flight path of the missile proclaimed, 'It was a miss." I didn't know what to do with myself. I had ruined the whole important deal. All eyes were on me and our Israeli-made missile, and our hope had gone down the drain because of one stupid miss. I felt tears rush to my eyes. Meanwhile, they were explaining to the Poles that it was an 'operating malfunction' a common term for such experiments, meaning that it was human error and not a problem with the missile itself.

"Anyway, it was decided that we would do another launch at once. I collected myself, wiped away the tears, and told myself, calm down, Gilad. You know what to do in these situations, you are the one who developed this missile and you know it well. Let go of all emotion and focus just on the tank simulation before you. I won't bother you with the story further, but the second launch was successful and the tank went up in flames at once. Everyone applauded from the benches, perhaps also because of the rumor that I myself was a son of survivors who had been at a camp not far from Skarzysko-Kamienna.

"That same day, the huge deal was signed between Mesko and Rafael Defense Systems, and the Polish press went out of its way to praise the great contribution of Israeli technology to Polish security.

"The head of the team hugged me and put his hand on my shoulder. 'You did it Gilad. It was obvious to me that you would get it, after all, 'Gil' is yours, you have been part of it since its beginning and there was no way you'd miss. It's understandable that you would be nervous on the first try. Only someone with a heart of stone wouldn't get overwhelmed by the situation.' By the way, just for general information, the official name of the 'Gil' missile is 'Spike.' All I could think about when the signing was over was how I would pass on all this excitement to Mom and Dad, waiting for me back in Israel. Dad, who had always told stories of his village, of the butcher and the shoemaker and the school teacher, and loved to read Shalom Aleichem, who reminded him of the world that had been erased. I felt that today I had come full circle. The generational circle of the Jews in the village before the war, and their proud, educated offspring, Israelis and their technological developments." Yula got up from her chair to hug Gilad and said, "We were like human dust, despised and humiliated into ash. Now, thanks to you and your teammates, we showed them: not only did you not eliminate us, but now you need our developments to strengthen your army. Thank you, Gilad." She planted a kiss on his cheek and sat down. Amos did not miss the opportunity to take a photo of the two heroes together.

"Sorry that I stole the stage here," said Gilad apologetically. "Now it's your turn. Please tell us the story you promised to tell. Here you are with us now, after everything you went through in that terrible camp, and all of it thanks to that huge dog who saved you."

"But first of all, this matter of the 'firings,' as they called it there," Yula continued her story. "When the body got weak and could no longer be of use, you would get terribly afraid. That's what happened to me in those summer days when the typhus epidemic was raging through the camp. The illness was extremely contagious. I got sick and lost weight and was practically a skeleton. Of course, I was unable to work, and every day I was afraid that they would take me to be shot because there was no crematorium to get rid of unnecessary workers. By some great miracle, they took me to one of the barracks that was assigned to the sick. They didn't really take care of the patients, just made sure that we didn't infect everyone else. And they were also afraid of lice. I remember the plague of lice that befell us again and again. We were full of them. We joked that we didn't have lice but rather, the lice had us. We would shower in cold water in the communal showers, the one in which I once met Sabina, when we first bonded.

Now, in the sick barracks, I met Danka who was more or less my age and also had typhus. They moved me to lie in the bed beside hers. We would dream together and tell one another about our childhoods. Danka wasn't from Warsaw but from a small town north of Warsaw. Both of us imagined and dreamed of oranges in the land of Israel. How we would eat an orange together, break it into two because there wasn't enough, and the juice would drip down our chins and chests, and the taste would be heaven. I didn't yet know what an orange even tasted like." Yula took a break for a moment and Amos said how much she loved citrus fruits, and oranges in particular, to this day. He added that when the season begins, he brings her great piles of oranges.

"But then, in those days, I was miserable," said Yula. "I had no appetite, and I was swollen with hunger. Weak, just skin and bones, barely forty kilos. When I was released from the quarantine barracks, after I was supposedly recovered from the typhus, I would just wander around the camp. Without purpose, because I couldn't work. I was sure that my end was near and that this time the Gypsy's magic would not help me. Every day seemed like my last. If not today, surely tomorrow they would take me out and shoot me. There were selections in advance of a new transport that was supposed to arrive, and every Monday and Thursday we all stood in formation for selection, where Dr. Rost and another doctor in charge of selection would pass among all of us and decide who stayed and who got on the truck."

Yula took a small sip from the cup of juice beside her.

"Here, I will tell you something that will illustrate the cynicism and the cruelty of the commanders there. In the winter, when rumors were coming from the white house about a new transport of healthy Jews that was supposed to arrive, new barracks were built and the old ones renovated and painted. New hope was planted in the prisoners' hearts. Everyone waited and wondered — what will happen? Who will stay, and who will go?

"One rainy morning, Dr. Rost and his deputy appeared along with the doctor, hunting the sick people who had received permission not to work and were wandering around the camp — like me just then — like *Muselmann*.[4] At the end of the hunt, they had caught some hundred and fifty sick people and the whole group was loaded onto trucks. When they passed by the kitchen, the trucks stopped. Nobody understood why, but they were allowed off the trucks, and there was great happiness because they thought that maybe Dr. Rost and his deputy had changed their minds. Apparently, the reason turned out that since they were officially registered among the camp's workers, they deserved to have lunch. Since it was exactly lunchtime when they brought the soup tureens to the distribution spot beside the kitchen, it was decided that each of the convicts would receive a nice portion of soup, and everyone relaxed and ate eagerly. Not half an hour had passed when the cynicism of the Germans revealed itself. 'Back to the trucks! Everybody, quickly now!' They commanded. Screams rose to the heavens. People fell to their knees and pleaded for their lives, but the Germans were only following orders, even cynical ones. Those who watched it happen said that even among the Germans and Polish soldiers who herded them back onto the trucks, there were some wiping away tears.

"Now you understand why I was afraid? They could give you soup with one hand and with the other push you onto a truck."

---

4   "*Muselmann*" was slang used by Jewish prisoners of Nazi concentration camps during the Holocaust (World War II) to refer to those suffering from a combination of starvation (known also as "hunger disease") and exhaustion, as well as those who were resigned to their impending death.

Yula took another short pause. Everyone was silent until Gilad asked, "But what happened on that fateful day when they did fire you? "

"Well, that day, I remember it was a hot summer day and I, like I said before, was wandering around the camp doing nothing. My hair was falling out and when I saw myself in the cracked mirror at the clinic, I thought that if they were sending the useless to the shooting range, then they would surely choose me. Suddenly I heard shouting.

"'*Appell, Appell*! Five minutes, everyone to the courtyard!' We all gathered, all of the *Muselmann* who remained at the camp, because the rest were at work. Maybe the Germans felt the end nearing and that the Russians were approaching. Dr. Rost, as serious as ever, arrived with his huge dog and his deputy, who passed between us pulling people out of the line, left and right. The way I looked, I was sent to the side of the people to be shot. I stood there overwhelmed by thoughts of the end. I tried to recall the good days with Mom and Dad, the vacation that summer at Helena's guest house, the meeting with the Gypsy who promised me, 'you will live to age ninety-three,' and my beautiful friend Barbara who was always by my side. And then I suddenly felt hot, humid air-like breath, which made it through the dirty paper that was my only clothing. I looked around and saw Ziggy. He wanted love and affection from me now? What could I give him a moment before they took me to the place from which nobody returns? Ziggy lay his head on me and howled softly. I heard a man's voice order, 'Lily, get up now.' It was Rost, who always called me 'Lily.' 'Come Lily, you're coming this way,' he declared and brought me to the lineup of the living.

"He must have looked for Ziggy and noticed him standing beside me, pointing his big nose at me, the wretch wrapped in old paper. I was so far from that Yula who had arrived at the camp a year earlier, but Ziggy recognized me. Maybe by my smell, or some other sense that some humans are missing, and the Germans and Poles had lost a long time ago: a sense of compassion. But thanks to Ziggy, Dr. Rost approached me, pulled me from the condemned, and sent me back to the living. Call it luck or call it fate. Or call it the love of a dog. My cousin used to say, 'Dogs and Jews don't go together. If you see a Jew with a dog, either the dog is not a dog or the Jew is not a Jew. One of the two.' Anyway, all I know is that since that incident, I have loved dogs with more passion and I love them to this day."

Yula grew silent and looked around at everyone. There wasn't a dry eye in the room and an oppressive silence prevailed. Suddenly Gilad broke the silence. "And after that? How did you get to Israel?"

"I will spare you the rest," said Yula. "The nightmare wasn't over yet. Rost transferred me to a different camp, to Buchenwald, where I worked closing naval mines until April 1945. Afterward, I took part in the Death March to Dresden and fled from there. I moved to Israel in 1948. Anyway, it's not for nothing they say that dogs are a man's best friend. Dogs bring love into the world."

15

Since the meeting, which had made waves at school, Tom was busy studying for exams, and with Efrat's help, he managed to stay in the honors math class. Meanwhile, Gilad's story and the story of Yula and the dog who saved her soon spread throughout the school.

For Holocaust Remembrance Day, the class was given an assignment to interview a Holocaust survivor or family member who had been through that terrible war. The assignment would be carried out in groups of two or three students and the subject, which their teacher chose for them, was "Childhood in the Ghetto." Tom, who had been listening to Yula's stories for some time, asked Efrat to join him and the two of them planned to complete the project as a team. This time, for a change, they would talk not about the camp but about childhood in the ghetto. Of course, Tom would have preferred to write about Ziggy, the dog who saved Yula and was her guardian angel. When Efrat and Tom arrived to meet at Yula's house, she welcomed them just as Zoya, her caregiver, brought her afternoon coffee and cookies.

"Have some," said Yula and began to tell them how just yesterday a young woman who was researching the subject of dogs in the Holocaust had called her. "She wanted to come and interview me about Ziggy, the Great Dane who saved me," said Yula. "Doesn't that seem strange to you? That someone is suddenly researching dogs in the Holocaust?" she asked, surprised.

"Why not?" Tom replied. "It's actually a fascinating subject. Surely not all of the dogs were vicious like Ziggy. There must have been others. I'm sure there were dogs who helped or even saved weak prisoners," said Tom, as if he knew what he was talking about. "Even Ziggy had his kind, compassionate side. Even though dogs are usually devoted to their owners and see them as the leader of the pack."

"What pack?" Yula asked.

"In nature, they live in packs," Tom replied. "And it's imprinted on them that there's a pack leader whose orders they follow. In this case, Dr. Rost."

"Never mind," said Yula. "In any case, I asked her if it might be possible to find a dog like that, like Ziggy, to bring him here, just for a bit, so I could pet him. A Harlequin one, the kind with white fur with black spots, like I described to you. That girl, her name is Tammy, said, 'Of course! You don't have to explain Harlequins to me, I am an expert in that breed,'" said Yula. "Anyway, don't be surprised if someday soon my dream comes true, and you find a dog like Ziggy sitting in my living room so I can pet him and thank him personally."

"Do you remember how I already found you a similar dog? I even brought you a picture and you said that it wasn't the dog you meant," said Tom, and pulled out the photo of the dog he had shown her before.

"He really is similar. The same breed. But you see how his coloring is more black and bluish?" Yula pointed at the photograph. "See?" She asked everyone in the room. "Rost's dog was a Harlequin. A similar size, but the colors and maybe even the personality are different. 'Harlequin' means 'clown,' and you can see that he's dressed in a clown costume with those spots. There's no way there isn't a single one of those in Israel."

"I'll keep looking," said Tom.

Yula encouraged him, "I don't care which of you is first to find one and bring him here, whether it's you or that researcher, that would be amazing."

"But meanwhile, I told you that we have a subject to prepare for Holocaust Memorial Day," said Tom. "And we wanted you to tell us something about the period in which you were a girl, our age approximately, in the ghetto."

"Our class was assigned to write a survivor's memories of childhood in the ghetto," said Efrat. "You know, Tom, I don't like the way people memorialize us and coddle us. For years, they have been bothering me, trying to put me back into the Holocaust survivor category, taking me back to that dark, blood-stained past," Yula said angrily.

"I'm sorry if the expression takes you back," said Efrat. "You're right that these days, the term gets thrown around without consideration for the person behind the survivor, who maybe suffers every time he or she is reminded of that terrible period of their life. You'd probably rather just live your normal life."

"That's what bothers me so much," said Yula. "Now I want my privacy and my normalcy, like everyone else. To enjoy my grandchildren and great-grandchildren. And stop reminding me of that all the time." "Okay. I see that I have burdened you enough," Yula sighed. "Why don't you have a cookie?"

Tom reached out his hand, took a cookie, and put it in his mouth.

"Good, now listen." Yula stretched out in her chair. "I was just thinking of something suitable for your subject. What comes to mind is the encounter I had one night with three members of the Jewish underground."

She began to tell her story and Tom pressed 'record' on his phone.

"These are the same members of the underground who later on were responsible for the Warsaw Ghetto Uprising in late April 1943. But this was about a year earlier, in 1942. I was sixteen years old then, a bit older than you, and the underground operatives were looking for collaborators…"

Tom looked at Yula in amazement. "Collaborators with the Germans? Were there people like that?" He asked in disbelief.

"There was a group of Jews like that called the 'Jewish Gestapo,' another organization called the 'Group of 13,' or 'Chinestka' in Polish. That was their nickname. They traded on the black market and other illegal things, but the worst was that they would inform on Jews who were hiding from the

Gestapo. There was a lot I did not know then, because I was a child, a young woman, and I only knew that this was a group whose members wore green hats in the street and their leader was a very handsome man but did terrible things.

"In that same period, I had a friend whose parents lived in the same building as my grandmother, on Poznanska Street. I would go over to her place sometimes where we would play together. I really loved going over there," said Yula, taking a sip of coffee before setting it down on the table.

"One day, when I was at her place, they had just declared a curfew. It was forbidden to leave the house, so I stayed and slept over at her place. At one in the morning, we heard pounding on the door. We were terribly frightened. 'They must have informed on us,' my friend said, and I saw that she, too, was shaking with fear, like me. Apart from her parents, there was another, quiet guy there with us, who always dressed well and wore a hat. His name was Furstenberg. He particularly liked me and would give me candies once in a while. It was said that he had connections to the black market, but nobody knew exactly what he did. After the pounding on the door, three men burst inside. They got us out of bed, shouting, and had us stand in the living room. I screamed with fear and one of the guys came up to me, grabbed me by the chin, and twisted my head. 'Be quiet, now,' he shouted. His name was Itzko, and he wore a beret on his head and had a sharp face. One of the other guys told him, 'Itzko, leave her alone,' in Polish, and introduced the three as members of the Jewish underground. He approached Furstenberg and asked him to take a step forward.

We were all standing, trembling with fear and cold, and didn't understand what was happening before us. Then, one of the underground guys pulled a crumpled piece of paper from his pocket, stood, and read the indictment of the Jewish underground against Yosef Furstenburg, as he was called, from the paper. We were shocked. From the indictment, we heard that he was accused of being a member of the 'Group of 13' as a liaison between the organization and the German Gestapo, and was responsible for the reporting of Jews to the Gestapo — at this point, they read a list of names — who were then executed by torture. When the reading was finished, one of the underground members, who had shouted at me to be quiet before, pulled a gun out of his belt, asked everyone to line up before him, and shot one bullet into Furstenberg's forehead. He fell, his head hit the floor, and a puddle of blood began to grow around his head. I wanted to scream but couldn't manage so much as a silent chirp.

"That was the first execution I witnessed in my life, and from our side. He did it professionally and in cold blood," she said. "I met those guys from the underground a few more times, later on. Itzko in particular, the one who shouted at me to be quiet. I remember him well, maybe because of the beret he wore.

"A year later the uprising broke out. It happened on the evening of Passover, April 1943, a year after my father was killed and the Germans bombed the ghetto from all sides, including the air. Everything was burning, all of the houses and attics. Members of the underground not only fought the Germans but also protected us and smuggled us from one attic to another to the next. I remember just moving between attics or basements. And the basements burned too. Itzko was quick with strong hands, and when he held mine, I felt safe. After spending a night in a dark attic, with the sounds of grenades exploding all around us, he appeared between clouds of smoke, took me by the hand again, and ran through a few dark basements until we found ourselves in a huge bunker, like out of a fairy tale. There was even a clean shower and bathroom there. The bunker was full of food. For years I hadn't seen amounts of food like at the Zamenhof Platz. I remember trying to taste everything. There was chicken, potatoes, and fruit, but we didn't get around to eating properly when suddenly everything filled with smoke and shouting in German, 'schnell, raus, schnell,' meaning, 'hurry, get out, quick.' We exited with our hands in the air. They must have been expecting tough militants because when we came outside, that same clear, sunny morning, we were surprised to see rows of armed German soldiers, aiming their rifles and even a machine gun at us. We looked wretched as we came out into the light of day. This time I really realized that our end was near and again panicked. I remember that I told my mother, 'What a beautiful day today, it's a shame to die on such a beautiful day.' And truly, for a young girl, who under different circumstances would be in the prime of life, the awareness that her life was ending now was too hard a blow to bear. In any case, in my heart of hearts, I held onto the hope that again someone above would look out for us. Again, I recalled the words of the old Gypsy woman in my head, who had read my lifeline and told me that I would live until ninety-three, and again I felt certain.

"We stood there in the spring sunlight, for maybe an hour or more, and in the end, they took us to the Umschlagplatz, to the train to Majdanek."

Tom couldn't restrain himself and asked, "And what about Itzko? Did they catch him too?"

"I never saw Itzko again. He brought us to the bunker and then disappeared," Yula said sadly. "Just when I got to Israel, I heard that he was killed during that same event. That's it, enough for today, I hope that I didn't burden you too much with my stories." She finished talking and called Zoya to take the cups from the side table.

Later, Tom searched on Google and realized that as few Great Danes as there were in all of Israel, there were even fewer Harlequins. Very few people kept Great Danes of that kind. That made the mission much more complicated, and when Tom managed to find a man with such a dog, it turned out that the dog was already very old and would soon die. The dog's owner suggested that Tom try the Israeli Great Danes club and ask them for assistance.

In the phone call with the secretary of the club, Meital Bar-Sela, she was surprised by the sudden interest in this particular, rare breed. "Suddenly everyone is interested in Harlequins. There are only five such dogs in the whole country and they're all over."

Tom realized that Tammy, the researcher that Yula had mentioned, must have called before he did. Meital, the secretary, was able to tell him that the researcher had come by her office and seemed very knowledgeable on the subject of dogs at the extermination camps and ghettos during the time of the Holocaust.

"For instance, she told me that in her research, she discovered that alongside the familiar stories of cruel dogs whose owners were German officers like the terrible Amon Goth, commander of the Plaszow Camp, there were other dogs who helped save Jews whose stories we still don't know. But what is your connection to the story? Are you her grandson or something? You sound young."

"Not her grandson, but I'm interested in the subject for my own reasons. I've been promising that same Holocaust survivor, Yula, for some time now that I would look for a Harlequin dog for her, like the one that saved her in the camp," said Tom, and then Meital told him that the club management was taking Yula's request seriously. "We've already recruited two huge Harlequins for that visit — one by the name of Nikita, and the other is Kim — who will come to Yula's home next week, with Tammy."

Two days before the meeting with the dogs at Yula's, Tom visited her. Yula was very excited. "You won't believe it!" She said excitedly when Tom arrived. "It's finally happening. I can't wait to meet and hug the Harlequin."

"Yes, I heard that from the club secretary I spoke to on the phone," said Tom. "I understand that you've already set a meeting. The main thing is that we will finally see this special dog face to face," he added, trying to hide his disappointment that he was unable to reach the club first.

"This is great, Tom. And just so you know, I really appreciate your efforts to bring me a dog like I asked. I understand that Tammy happened to know someone from the Great Danes club, which is how they managed to arrange not one, but two to come visit. Two Harlequins, who will come visit me on Wednesday! Finally, I will get to pat a dog like Ziggy," she said. "You don't know how much warmth and love such a huge dog like Ziggy can give," she added with a big hand gesture. "Just a ball of love, this dog. I am excited already. And you're invited, too, of course. And bring Efrat with you, I really like her." When the dogs came that afternoon, it was like a holiday at Yula's house. It was just a few days before her ninety-fourth birthday and she was going to get the gift for which she had been waiting for so long. She sat in her chair in the living room, the same chair in which she always sat when she told Tom her stories from the camp, but this time by her side sat Kim, an enormous Harlequin dog, just like she had described Ziggy in her stories: a dog whose head, even when sitting, reached the chair's armrest. Yula reached her hand out to pet the white fur decorated with black spots of all sizes. It was clear that Yula was enjoying petting her and kept saying, "Now this is a dog," emphasizing 'this,' as if to say that only a dog of this size, and with such intelligent eyes, could be considered a real dog. And it was evident that Kim was also enjoying Yula's caresses and made that same lip-smacking *"tze... tze... tze..."* sound that she knew to do to summon Dingo to her and Ziggy too.

Now, both Harlequins sat on either side of her in the small living room and didn't understand what all the fuss around them was about. Amos photographed and Anat brought out refreshments for the guests. Among the guests was Sharon, the owner of Nikita, who was restless, unlike her friend Kim. On that day, Yula celebrated what she had been waiting for for so long, and again told the story to those present of the special connection that she had with Ziggy, the dog that so terrified the prisoners. All of the girls who had been with Yula in the worst department of the whole camp, 'Werk C,' warned her not to dare approach that terrible dog. Again and again, she told how, against all odds, the connection between them grew closer, and the dog looked out for her and brought her pieces of sausage that he received from Dr. Rost, while hunger at the camp was unbearable and prisoners would fight over a piece of bread or a half-rotten potato that they found in the field.

Until that eventual miracle at the end, when she was already a shadow of herself and weighed only thirty-two kilograms, barely recovering from the typhus that left her body and mind unfit for physical work and an obvious candidate to be fired in the way from which nobody returns. It was then that her guardian angel appeared in the form of the dog Ziggy, and changed her fate when he pressed his nose against her in her paper suit. Ziggy indicated to his master, Dr. Rost, who was supervising the selection process, to take her out of the line of those condemned to die. And when she heard the commanding voice of Dr. Rost calling her, "Lily, come here. Lily, you're going this way," and moved her to the line of the living, she understood that thanks to Ziggy, she had been saved, and she pet his head lovingly. Her mouth was so dry from fear that she was unable to make her lip-smacking sound to him as she moved to the line of the living.

Anat stopped beside Tom and Efrat with a tray of cakes. Tom reached out and took a slice, and Efrat made a polite head gesture to indicate 'no' and said only "thanks" in a weak voice. Later she explained to Tom that she was so riveted by Yula's story she couldn't imagine eating anything.

16

When Gilad returned to the school after his trip, he discovered that a bad quarrel had broken out between two of the classes in his absence. He managed to take control of the situation that nearly turned violent, and he managed to unite everyone around the national competition which would take place two weeks later at the Nokia Center.

The quarrel began between two of the tenth-grade classes (10B and 10C) while Gilad was away. Class 10 C discovered a malfunction in their Roboner, which they had worked so hard on. One day it ran into the labyrinth wall and remained stuck for a long time. Until then, 10C's robot was thought to be invincible, and now the 10C team, led by the talented Alon, was at a loss and began to blame the 10B team for intentional sabotage.

Someone from Alon's team claimed to have seen Eviatar from 10B walking around the rival class' table after everyone had dispersed and gone home last Monday, and rumor had it that he had sabotaged the robot's delicate mechanism.

Harsh words were exchanged, and the two sides nearly came to blows. Eviatar swore on everything dear to him that he had not been there and certainly had not touched their robot.

"The Roboner competition in two weeks at the Nokia Center in Tel Aviv is between schools, not between teams," Gilad told his students in a quiet voice. "It would be a shame to sabotage your own school's chance of winning the national competition. You have a good chance and it would win us tickets to participate in the international competition in Hartford, Connecticut. So, no more fighting."

It didn't take long for Gilad to realize what was wrong with 10C's robot. It was a software error. One of the programs, the one responsible for decoding the transmission that came from one of the sensors, had gone into an infinite loop because of a counter someone on their team had forgotten to reset.

"Nobody went into 10C's program to disrupt anything," said Gilad. "It was human error, which could happen to anyone. So no more suspicion and blame, please."

Gilad went on to explain that these kinds of programming mistakes could happen even when everything was working well. Whenever someone tried to improve a feature in a program, even if it was unrelated to the rest of the coding which was working fine, they had to check again to make sure that they didn't forget to reset any newly defined counter.

"These are simple, but frustrating things," he said, "But you can't lose your head, and certainly not blame the other team right away. First, check it out yourselves. Run the programs again and see. Haste and emotion will not help you."

Then he told everyone about the "Gil" missile whose development was done in his department where he was the team development leader, and how when emotions interfered with trying to focus on the target, he could miss. "That's exactly what happened to me in the middle of our presentation of the missile's capabilities. It was a critical presentation, and I actually remembered what my father told me before I left on the delegation to Poland: 'Remember that you are representing the Jewish people,' he said. 'The same people that had once not been worth the dirt on their shoe are now developing military technology that the Polish military officers are interested in."

From that day on, the two teams worked together under Gilad's guidance and even put in overtime hours to meet the stringent competition requirements. Tom, who was part of the 10B team's efforts, was very interested in the subject and improved his programming skills. But he also had to make time to study for his assessment exams in geography and history.

He didn't see Efrat as much, and when he did, they no longer took Dingo out on walks together.

"You'll see, everything will change after the competition," he promised. "I'm really busy with this project just now."

"I admire your dedication," said Efrat. "But you have to find time for walks and friends, too. If you carry on like this, there's no point in us going out."

As the date of the competition approached, the teams grew increasingly tense. Luckily, Gilad knew how to keep everyone calm. He would move between the teams, making improvements in speed and precision. Sometimes there was just a technical problem, like a fan that was supposed to blow out the candle, and Gilad knew how to fix it.

On the day of the competition, the teams were nervous and excited. Both teams, 10B and 10C, would represent the Givolim School from Ramat Gan. Everyone believed that their robot would perform well. But, as in any competition, they were also afraid that the other schools might be better. The parents were invited as guests, and like with many recent school events, Eleanor, Tom's mother, was absent.

The Nokia Center was crowded and bustling as if it were an important soccer game. All of the guests sat in rows of chairs higher up in the stand while the competing teams, school representatives, teachers and instructors, sat below. The labyrinths were in place on the wooden floor, simulating the walls and rooms of an apartment in which the Roboner was meant to complete its task of recognizing and then extinguishing a candle. Touching the walls would not disqualify teams, but it would lose them points.

The tension was great. The announcer read out the names of the schools participating in the competition. There were some teams in which two schools had joined together, like the Misgav school from the Galilee, which had joined the ORT Binyamina school. In each heat, two teams competed against one another. The announcer read out the rules, with the time starting from the moment the bell rang until the successful extinguishing of the candle and the robot's return to its starting point. This also determined scoring.

Gilad's team from the Givolim school was drawn for the heat against Ein Shemer Iron regional school. It was a close competition and tensions were high. Both groups' fans were shouting encouragement and there was a tense moment when the Ein Shemer Roboner got stuck on one of the corners and couldn't move forward. Even though the judges were understanding and allowed for a timeout, the Ein Shemer students were unable to get their Roboner unstuck. The Ein Shemer friends and parents could be heard groaning with disappointment mingled with the enthusiastic cheering from the Givolim crowd. The Ein Shemer team's bad luck was that their Roboner got stuck after it had already managed to successfully put out the candle before the Givolim Roboner even made it to theirs. The Ein Shemer team was disqualified and Givolim won by default.

In the second round, the Givolim team competed against ORT Hadera, and this time both groups' Roboners managed to make smooth progress, without any errors, but the Givolim Roboner was faster and more efficient, and they had a clear win.

From one stage to the next, Gilad's team was moving up to qualify for the tournament finals. The Misgav and ORT Binyamina joint team also qualified for the finals against Givolim's 10B team. Everyone was nervous up until the sound of the gong which broke the tense silence, but from that moment on, the crowd was roaring. But as their robot neared the final goal, two more turns to the candle, Tom noticed that the

Givolim Roboner's right wheel was starting to come loose. Tom, who noticed the problem in time, asked Gilad to declare a time out for them. In the few seconds he had, Tom quickly screwed the wheel back on tightly and managed to stabilize the Roboner. They reached the candle, extinguished it, and had just three more corners to turn to win, but they accidentally touched a wall during one of the turns which lost them five points so that in the end, it was a tie between Givolim and Misgav. Both teams won the coveted trophy and the tickets to the international competition in Hartford, Connecticut. Tom was also applauded by the Givolim fans, 'he's a hero, Tom is a hero!' For his close attention and fixing the malfunction in time.

After their victory, Tom's father hugged him warmly and was exuberant, but Tom was distracted, wondering why his mother had not come. He was going to ask his father about it but thought perhaps the question would embarrass him. He was bothered by his mother's strange behavior lately. She often shut herself in her room and was almost never in the same room with his father. Tom did not overthink it. After all, they had always been two quite different people, each with their own interests, but the silence at home was becoming increasingly worrying. He recalled what Efrat had said about her parents, but disregarded any comparison. Efrat was also among the fans from the school and now she waited for him beside the main exit. She hugged him and gave him a kiss on the cheek. They walked hand in hand toward the parking lot.

"Are you coming over?" He asked, as if it were obvious.

"Sure, of course. My mom didn't wait for me here, she just dropped me off," said Efrat.

The two sat quietly in Reuben's car until they got home. From a distance, Tom already noticed the yellow ambulance waiting by the building's entrance. They got out of the car and ran toward it. Two paramedics in white were already pushing a stretcher on wheels. As they got closer, they saw Amos walking beside it carrying a small bag and understood that it was Yula on the stretcher and Amos was carrying a bag with a few of her things that she would need. Amos was anxiously asking the paramedic who held the ventilator to her mouth, "How serious is it?" to which the paramedic replied, "It will be alright, dear."

They pushed the stretcher up the ramp into the ambulance. "Can I come with you?" Amos asked after they slammed the back door closed. "It's better if you come in your own car," one of the paramedics suggested. "That way you will be more mobile," he added and got in. Amos remained standing and barely noticed that Tom and Efrat had appeared beside him.

"Heart attack," Amos told them. "It was sudden. This afternoon I noticed that she was breathing heavily and at first I didn't think much of it; I thought that she was tired from her walk, but when she said she felt pressure in her chest, I called an ambulance at once." He took his car keys from his pocket, saying, "Excuse me. I have to go to the hospital now. There's no time," and turned to the row of parked cars.

Reuben went into the house and came out with Dingo on his leash.

"Come with me, let's let Dingo out a bit. I haven't been out with him in a while because of the competition," Tom said to Efrat.

They walked hand in hand on their usual path, not far from the Yarkon, and went up to their knoll as Dingo walked ahead of them, pulling on the leash every time a butterfly or bird passed by.

"I thought that at his age he would have stopped his childish habit of chasing birds," Tom said as he pulled hard on the leash to bring Dingo back toward him. "It's more puppy behavior and he's already grown up, but maybe he still has some of his curiosity."

"Like you, Tom," Efrat said. "You are also really curious and excited by every new discovery."

They sat in their usual spot on the knoll. The red sun sank beyond the towers of Tel Aviv, Efrat rested her head on Tom's lap and said, "Do you also sometimes think about how complicated our world is?" Tom looked pensive and didn't reply.

"Are you even listening?" She raised her voice.

"Yes," he said. "Complicated is not the word. On the one hand, I was so happy about the victory today and everyone was proud of me, but on the other hand, Yula is in the hospital. At least this time it isn't my fault. And the situation between my parents isn't great," he added sadly as he threw a small stone that he had picked up from the ground.

"Yeah," said Efrat. "I noticed that your mom wasn't there today."

"That's true," Tom said sadly. "I feel like she is at a distance from what's happening at home. There's some kind of tension between her and my dad."

"I really get that, Tom," said Efrat. "I remember those days myself. I didn't know if I needed to take a side. I just remember that suddenly my dad became extra concerned and attentive to me, in a way he wasn't before," she sunk into her thoughts. "He tried so hard that he would even suggest driving me to activities at times when I didn't even have them. At first, I didn't understand why he was being so anxious."

"I hope that they're not there," said Tom, and a spark of hope lit up his eyes. "Maybe it's just a passing thing. Anyway, there was the crisis of moving to the city and all that."

"I still hope that it really all works out for the best," said Efrat. "Even though my mom would say that if it's not working then it won't work and it's a waste of time and money for mediators and therapists."

"It sounds like your mom was really decisive about these things," said Tom when they reached the traffic light on the corner.

"Just realistic," she said. "But maybe your family is different and there really isn't anything to worry about," she said gently, hugging him around the shoulders and resting her head against him. "Remember, Tom, I'm always here. In good and bad."

Warmth and affection lit up Tom's eyes as he looked at her. "Come on, let's keep going," he said, embarrassed, as the light turned green. Then he held her hand and the two crossed the street. They returned right as Maya, Efrat's mother, arrived.

"Well, how did it go?" She asked.

"Tom was amazing!" Said Efrat enthusiastically. "Their team is going to Hartford, Connecticut!"

"Wow, that's a huge accomplishment," said Maya. "Would you join them?" She asked Efrat.

"Of course, if it were possible," replied Efrat as she opened the car door.

"Meanwhile, you will have to make do with Ramat Gan," said Maya.

Efrat hugged him goodbye before getting into the car. "See you at school tomorrow," she called to him from the window as the car drove away.

Tom went home and let Dingo off his leash. The house was dark. He knocked lightly on his parents' bedroom door. Since he didn't hear any response, he opened the door a crack and peered inside. His father sat on the bed, his elbows resting on his knees and holding his head between his hands in a familiar position.

"Come in, Tom," Reuben whispered. "Your mother and I want to talk to you." As Tom entered the room, he saw his mother, Eleanor, standing beside the bed wearing her favorite dress, which she bought when they had just arrived in the city. She was wearing high-heeled shoes, not her usual sneakers, and her hair was tied back. She was holding a small trolley suitcase in one hand and looked like she was about to leave.

"What exactly is going on here?" Tom asked in surprise.

"That's exactly what we wanted to talk to you about. Please sit down," his father replied. Tom sat hesitantly.

"This discussion will be hard." He paused briefly, tilted his head, and stared at the floor. "Your mother and I are separating."

"Just like that? Out of nowhere?" Tom asked. He looked angrily at his mother and added, "You don't tell me anything and then just out of nowhere...?"

"You're right. But it's not so sudden," said Eleanor.

"I'm not even talking about discussing it with me, but at least you could have waited to say goodbye," Tom was furious. "I'm your son, no? Or are you so preoccupied with yourself that you forgot...?"

"You're right, Tom, you are our son, your father's and mine and we love you so much. But I am a mother who never knew how to be a mother," she said, her voice trembling. "And yes... I waited for you. My flight to New York doesn't leave until one in the morning. I wanted us to talk, heart to heart, and to tell you that sometimes I may have been harsh with you but that was never because I didn't love you. Maybe because I didn't know how to show love."

"I'm not mad, Mom, just sad. I'm so sad," said Tom in almost a whisper. "I tried to be good, I really tried," he added and then got up from the bed and paced the room until he stood facing her. "I so wanted you to be together. Like all parents. Of course, it's different in the city than the village. Most of my friends from class, their parents are not together."

"You were just fine, Tom," Reuben raised his head and spoke. "It has nothing to do with you. You didn't need to try or do anything, it's just about your parents, the relationship between your mother and me." Reuben stood and held Tom around the shoulders. He pulled him close and lovingly stroked his neck. Now he looked his son in the eye and went on, "These are things that happen in time, it isn't sudden. You must have noticed that things haven't been working so well lately," he said and sat back down on the bed.

Eleanor pulled her makeup chair from beside the big mirror and sat down across from Reuben. "Come, you sit too, Tom," she said as Tom sat down beside his father, "When you were little, and we were in the village, everything was still fine," she said in a conciliatory voice. "I thought I would get over it, but it was really hard for me in the village. And as time went on, it became hard for me to stay here, too."

"I know," said Tom. "After all, we came to the city for you, so you would feel better here."

"Yes, I'm sorry, even the move didn't work."

"Yes," Reuben added, sadly, "We've talked a lot about this, your mother and I. Even before we moved here, I always said that if something wasn't working for you, or with us, a change of location wouldn't fix it. There's a saying, 'change of place, change of fortune,' but it doesn't always work. You carry everything with you, who you are and your problems, to whatever new place, too."

"Your father was right, Tom, and I'm so sorry. I know that I wasn't there for you," she said. "And you shouldn't have had to pay the price."

"I'll be okay, Mom. I am not the only one in this situation," said Tom and cast his eyes down.

"I just hope that when you're older you'll understand me better," she said. "Dad and I came from different worlds. It just didn't work between us. As much as we tried to keep up our relationship, and not just for you, we thought we had to keep up the spark that was once there. But that spark never really grew into a full flame," she said sadly.

"So what will we do now?" Tom asked. "What will you do, Mom? And what about you?" He turned to his father. "And what about me?"

"I might try to return to the village. That depends on you," said Reuben. Tom was stunned by what he had heard. After everything that had happened with him here, would they go back to the village?

"I don't think I want to go back, Dad," said Tom. "I like it here now." He turned to his mother, "You don't even know that our school team won the robotics competition today."

"And you won't believe our Tom's resourcefulness, it's thanks to him they won," said Reuben."

"What? That was today?" Eleanor asked in surprise. "I was so busy with my own matters, I completely forgot about it."

"And we didn't just win, my team will represent Israel in the international competition in Hartford, Connecticut next month."

"Really? In America?" She said excitedly.

"Yes, and there was some kind of problem like Dad mentioned before. If I hadn't noticed on time, we wouldn't be going."

"I always knew that you see things that others don't and that you have something special, Tom," said Eleanor. "I'm so happy for you." She appeared to wipe away a tear.

"When I was little and we were still in the village, you didn't think of me like that then... You yelled at me all the time. I would pray for a different mom."

"Seriously?" She marveled, half laughing. "I don't recall that I yelled at you so much."

"Yeah, there was that one time in particular, when I wanted to scare you as a joke and I brought you two dead rats from the turkey coop."

"Oh, those turkeys, don't remind me. Maybe that's one of the reasons I had to get out of there. It was terrible! The dirt, the smell, and the noise. Ugh!" She grimaced in disgust. "At least if it had made money! But it didn't even do that," she said. Then, turning to Reuben, she added, "That's not your fault, Reuben, that I am allergic to those smells."

"It's not just the smells," said Reuben. "You always yelled that we never made a penny from them," now Reuben raised his voice. "You would get mad at me that it didn't turn a profit, but you didn't know how much money went to the merchants and the agents." He was quiet a moment and then said, "Forget it, we aren't here to fight over the past now. The time for reckoning has passed."

"See, Tom?" Eleanor said in a low voice. "There were big misunderstandings between us, right Reuben? And when we were younger, the passion of youth managed to cover over the gaps." Tom noticed the big, clear tear that rolled down her cheek. Her eyes were wet. She held out a hand to him and stroked his face, running her fingers through his hair. "I am so happy it went well, Tom, I'm so proud of you. It's a shame I wasn't there with you."

"Yeah we missed you there," Tom said.

"Yes, I'm self-absorbed sometimes, and then I don't see the forest for the trees…"

"Some of the fault is mine. I was always busy at work, maybe I even went there as a kind of refuge," Reuben said sadly. "And when you don't work on it, love fades. It's not good when two people live together under one roof when there's no longer anything between them."

"So what about you?" Tom asked his mother. "Are you going to Philly?"

"Yes, Tom, I am going back to the neighborhood I was born in. It's a hard thing to be torn from the place and the culture you were born in."

"Right," Tom said. "It's been like that for me, too. At first, you didn't understand why I was so miserable when we moved here, but now I like it and I actually prefer to stay."

"It was pretty clear to me," said his father.

"I'm happy for you," Eleanor told Tom. "It was a healthy process for you. I'm the one who's still stuck."

She held his hand in hers and said, "We have another hour or so until the taxi comes. Come, I'll make us dinner in the meantime." They managed to have a final meal together. At first, they ate in silence. Then the atmosphere warmed up and they spoke of their future plans. Eleanor told them that a childhood friend of hers would be waiting for her in the neighborhood where she grew up, and maybe she would sign up for a master's degree in the Philosophy of Art, a field she had always wanted to study. Reuben said that in the meantime he was in no hurry to make any decisions. First, Tom should finish his studies and afterward, all options were on the table, including returning to the village. He had even checked the rental contract and asked the tenants if they wanted to extend, because he was considering returning. Tom burst in then and said, "I am not a yo-yo that you can just play with as you like," he said angrily. "I also have a say in this." They fell into a tense, brief silence.

"After everything I've been through here at the beginning, now I like it here and I want to stay in this house."

Reuben set down his cup of tea on the table, wiped his mouth, and said, "This is probably about Efrat. Not that I'm opposed, but that doesn't have to be a reason. I really like her, by the way. From the first moment."

"It's not just Efrat," said Tom. "Lots of things have happened in the short time we've been here. It's hardly been a year, and I've learned so much."

Eleanor said what she always said in such situations, in English, of course, "Home is where the heart is."

"And what do you do when your heart is in two places?" Tom asked.

The taxi arrived at exactly nine-thirty and Tom and his father walked Eleanor to the car. Reuben carried the big suitcase and Tom took the little trolley suitcase. They parted with a hug. Tom noticed that both of them had tears in their eyes.

"Have a good time there, in Philadelphia, and may you finally be happy. Let us know how the flight went and everything," Reuben said to Eleanor and turned to go, maybe so that she wouldn't see how emotional he was.

Tom hugged his mother close and did not cry, just said that she should be strong and find her heart. And when she hugged him close, he felt that her cheek was wet.

That same evening Tom called Amos to ask about Yula.

"They took her to put in a catheter not long ago," Amos said in practically a whisper. He must have been somewhere with poor reception or where people weren't allowed to speak on the phone.

"It's not a great time to talk, call me back tomorrow," he said and hung up.

That night, Tom had a hard time falling asleep. Many things had happened that day. He thought primarily of his mother's departure and his upcoming trip to the competition in Hartford. Maybe he could meet her there, or she could come to the competition. He thought of Yula, too, who was once again in the hospital. He recalled what he had told Efrat about their complicated world.

The next day, Amos informed him that everything was fine, the catheterization had been successful, and Yula would return home in two days.

17

On the day that Yula returned home from the hospital, Tom came to visit and brought her a big bouquet of flowers. Yula was already sitting in her armchair and told him about her experience at the hospital.

"It's always harder the first time. You don't know what to expect," she said. "I remembered that last time when I was there with the leg fracture, it was different. I recalled that curfew in the ghetto when I hid inside that pile of snow and was so scared, I wet myself. Remember that I told you that story, Tom?" She turned to him and asked. "And do you remember what calmed me down in that pile of snow, and then again when I was waiting for the anesthesia at the hospital?"

Tom thought for a few seconds before remembering. "Of course. It was that old Gypsy woman's promise in the village, when she read your palm and saw your lifeline and said that you would live until ninety-three. Right?"

"Exactly," said Yula.

"But what happened with him, with the dog, Ziggy, in the end? Do you know?" Tom was curious to know.

"Actually, it just so happens that I found out that I was lucky to be saved from one of the final selections. The Russians were already very close, that's what Zhota told me, who remained there after I left and also turned out to be fortunate," said Yula as she tried to recall if it had indeed been Zhota who stayed on after her. "Never mind, someone who was there after I left told me that he killed him."

"Who killed who?" Tom asked in surprise.

"Dr. Rost, he killed his dog that he loved so much. The dog that he called 'Mensch.' He just shot him once in the head, the way he used to do to the prisoners, when he realized that all was lost and it was just a matter of days before the Russians would arrive," she said. "The Germans didn't want to leave any evidence behind. And Ziggy was at risk, or so Dr. Rost must have thought, and didn't want them to abuse him. He really did love that Mensch of his. He didn't call him that for nothing. He treated him like a person and us like dogs. When the day came, he wanted to show his beloved dog some mercy and not leave him in the hands of cruel soldiers. And there was a certain truth in that. In the end, the Russians turned out to be no less cruel than the Germans."

Tom thought for a moment then said, "But what was Ziggy guilty of? Why did Rost decide for him that it would be dangerous to remain at the camp?"

"Sometimes there's no choice, Tom. I also love dogs, as you know, but sometimes in life, you find yourself in situations that require tough choices. Even in the life of a dog, as in that of a person."

"I don't know what I would do if Dingo was in such a situation."

"Tom, when you write my story, just make sure you write about that awful camp, Skarzysko-Kamienna. Everyone needs to know what a horrific place it was. A place where the earth was soaked with Jewish blood," she said. "And remember Zhota, too, and Sabina, the only friends I had there. Maybe Danka, too, the one with whom we shared that dream about oranges in the land of Israel, even though I will never forget how in the end she married that doctor who wouldn't treat my mother when she was ill, just because we didn't have any money. Don't write about her. But promise me you will write about Gilad. His story about the missile moved me, and the deal that took place there, in that very camp. It's important to me that they know that he showed the big Polish army how a people, who were nearly annihilated, shook themselves off and built their own country, which creates technology that the Poles alone would never be able to produce.

"Promise me," she said.

"I promise," Tom replied and stood up from his seat. "Sorry, but I have to go. I'm supposed to meet Efrat now."

"Bring her tomorrow, I'd be happy to have a visit from both of you," she said before he closed the door.

Epilogue

The story you just read was based upon Nina Dinar Zinger, Yula's character in the book. Nina was born in Warsaw in 1926. She immigrated to Israel in 1948 at the age of twenty-two. Today, she lives in Kiryat Ono and has two children, five grandchildren, and two great-grandchildren.

In her youth, Nina went through all of the horrors of the war, beginning with the ghetto and the Umschlagplatz, via Majdanek, the work camp Skarzysko-Kamienna, Buchenwald, until the death march to Dresden from which she managed to escape. These places are landmarks of the evil and cruelty of the Nazis. I chose to focus on the work camp Skarzysko-Kamienna and Nina's story of being saved by the Harlequin Great Dane. That dog could be both terrifying as well as compassionate, two opposite traits coexisting within the same dog. The Great Dane, a dog bred for many years for hunting wild boars, became friendly to humans over time and very loyal to their masters, but suspicious of strangers. They are easily trained and obedient, and if trained to attack humans, they will do so at the command of their master. Evidently, the Germans brought the dogs already trained for their needs, as Meital Bar-Sela, the secretary at the Israel Great Danes' Club explained.

The incident when Nina was saved is a true story, which gives its readers the chills. The notion of 'the chills' is usually reserved for things that make your blood run cold but in Nina's story — or Yula, as she is called in the book — in the midst of all the horror and evil, there is a story of love between the dog of a camp commander, Dr. Rost, who counted and selected people to live or die, and Nina, the prisoner who is wasting away at the camp, living in constant fear that maybe today would be her last because she didn't meet her quota or she was absent from work.

It's worth noting that while Yula is based on Nina, she is not an exact copy of the real woman, but rather a literary character constructed from a collection of experiences and events as well as things not necessarily said and thought by her, but by other young women who survived the camp. When I first encountered this story in the Facebook group "Revenge of the Archive," a group of history enthusiasts, it made me tingle in horror and excitement at once; it was impossible to remain indifferent. In my case, Nina's story was my inspiration to write. From the moment that I decided to write the story of Nina and the dog, I felt that the task would not be so simple. I suspected that Nina would not easily offer information. Even in our first conversation, she expressed that I, as someone who was born in Israel and had not experienced the horrors of the war, couldn't understand, and certainly couldn't write about the people and events that they went through during those dark times. Nina doesn't like publicity or prying through everything related to that shocking period of the war. There was just one thing that she wanted and that she requested: to meet a Great Dane, like the one who saved her, once more. Then Tammy Bar-Yosef, who has been researching the subject of dogs in the Holocaust in recent years, came along and made Nina's dream come true. Tammy's research tells of the extensive negative use of dogs by the Nazis against Jews, but there are also lesser-known stories of dogs saving Jews, which was how she met Nina. In her meeting with Nina, assisted by Meital Bar-Sela, the secretary of the Israeli Great Dane Society, and Sharon Ronen, a dog drainer, were able to locate two Harlequin dogs for Nina, just like the kind Dr. Rost had for his cruel uses. "Just like the one that saved me in the Holocaust," Nina said and smiled happily as she embraced, caressed, and patted the backs of the two huge Harlequin dogs who sat in her living room in honor of her ninety-fourth birthday. Such a dog gave Nina the gift of mercy and now, in that meeting, she gave back love, not to the same exact dog, but a similar dog, that only people who understand dogs and can have such a special connection with them will understand. For Nina, that hug and caress symbolized the love between man and dog, and in her case, it was her way of saying thank you to the dog that saved her life.

Now, I wish to thank Nina Dinar, whose amazing character inspired me to write the book.

Thank you to Tammy Bar-Yosef, researcher of dogs in the Holocaust, whose work brought her to Nina and made her story known.

Thank you to Ronit and Yaakov Tzadikov, and to Nava Gigi, through whose book "Look After Sabina, Mom Said," I was acquainted with Sabina's special character.

To Meital Bar-Sela from the Israeli Great Danes Club, who opened my eyes to all things concerning this amazing breed of dogs.

And finally, thank you to the late Felicja Karay for the historical documentation of the camp in her book "Death Comes in Yellow."

Shmuel David
Tel Aviv, 2021

Printed in Great Britain
by Amazon